Whispers Of The Soul

A Journey Through Love, Loss, and Light

ED BREEDVELD

Whispers Of The Soul: A Journey Through Love, Loss, and Light © Ed Breedveld 2025

The moral rights of Edward Breedveld to be identified as the author of this work have been asserted in accordance with the Copyright Act 1968.

First published in Australia 2025 by Bovercon

ISBN 978-0-6457893-2-4

Any opinions expressed in this work are exclusively those of the author and are not necessarily the views held or endorsed by the Publisher.

All rights reserved. No part of this publication may be reproduced or transmitted by any means, electronic, photocopying or otherwise, without prior written permission of the author.

Disclaimer

All the information, techniques, skills and concepts contained within this publication are of the nature of general comment only and are not in any way recommended as individual advice. The intent is to offer a variety of information to provide a wider range of choices now and in the future, recognising that we all have widely diverse circumstances and viewpoints. Should any reader choose to make use of the information herein, this is their decision, and the author and publisher/s do not assume any responsibilities whatsoever under any conditions or circumstances. The author does not take responsibility for the business, financial, personal or other success, results or fulfilment upon the readers' decision to use this information. It is recommended that the reader obtain their own independent advice.

Dedication

To everyone who has inspired me and believed in me.

Contents

Introduction 1

Marks Of Love 5

   Love From A Distance 6

   The Welcoming 7

   The Guardian Angel 8

   A Poem For Ruby 10

   A Toast to Life 11

   Time 12

   Chain-Smoking Memories 14

   The Promise 16

   A Poem for Penny 17

   My Plea 18

   The Decision 20

   Connections 22

   My Wonderful Sons 23

   When Words Fall Short 24

   Friends 25

   Mama 26

   Self-made - For Lexi 28

   A Poem for Barbara 30

   The New Morning 31

My Love, My Soul Mate, My Destiny	32
The Brave Survivor – A Poem for Tracey	34
Just Till the Morning	36
My Promise To You	37

Moments Of Transcendence 39

The Beauty of a Woman	40
Nightly Reunion	42
The Ocean	43
Free	44
The Touch of Music	46
A Gift of Sight Beyond	47
Pavlova	48
My Plight	50
The Meeting Place	52
The Encounter	53
Going Home	54
Sweet Sounds	56
A Poem For Afia	57
The Healer	58
The River	60
A Daughter's Love	62
For My Love	64
For a Great Woman	65
Love Complete	66

Whispering Dreams 68

An Evening of Love 70

Bikers 72

A Lover's Verse 73

Shadows Within **75**

The Loss 76

The Man Within 77

For Kyle 78

The Unexpected Meeting 80

The Memory 82

The Jerk 84

A Father's Loss 85

The Truth 86

Leaking Love 88

Questions 89

The Final Ride 90

The Fleeting Memory 91

A Poem on True Beauty 92

Cold Realisation 94

The Mask 96

The Beast Within 98

The Returned Soldier 100

Distant Shores 101

A Poem for Her 102

- The Game 104
- The Familiar Ride 106
- Like Driftwood In The Ocean 107
- Angels on Earth 108
- Pushed Too Far 110

Other Places 113
- Blowing Winds 114
- From Despair 116
- The Cappuccino Sea 118
- Together Again 119
- Love Waiting 120
- Clinical Moment 122
- The Reunion 124
- Time To Say Goodbye 125
- The Old Soldier 126
- The Memory Train 128
- Midnight Caller 130
- The Cloaked Figure 132
- Answering the Call 133
- The Gatekeeper 134
- A Poem For My Passing 136
- A Mother's Love 137
- The Message 138
- The Return Visit 140

Glimpses 141

Quiet Thoughts 142

The Funeral 143

The Great Aussie Sick Day 144

Try Wearing His Clothes...146

The Tortured Soldier...148

Blowing Winds..150

From Despair 152

Words Of Hope **155**

The Unknowing Lighthouse..156

My Thoughts..158

The Torment 159

A Caring Heart...160

My Offer of Healing 162

My Life...164

The Quiet Places by Ed Breedveld..166

Is It Fair to Dream You Into Being?.. 167

My Life in Sail...168

The Gift 170

Life's Wonderous Journey 171

A Poem for Lily..172

Thoughts of Hope..174

The Healing..175

Prosperities Anchor 176

The Silent Conversation 177
The Drums Within 178
Ode To A Hero 179
The Hardest Journey 180
A Poem of Hope 182
The Secret of Life 184
My Birthday Poem 185
Breathe 186
My Life In A Book 188
Angels 190

Short stories 193
Undying Love 194
The Veil of Night 197

Conclusion 200
Acknowledgements 201
About The Author 202

Introduction

In this volume of my works, I have once again delved into the profound challenges, trials, and tribulations we are all inevitably subject to on this remarkable journey we call life. Life, with its unpredictable twists and turns, often brings with it moments of confusion, pain, and uncertainty. Yet, it also offers profound opportunities for growth, healing, and renewal.

Through these pages, my aim is not merely to share my thoughts or experiences but to extend a compassionate hand to those who find themselves struggling, lost, or overwhelmed by the weight of their circumstances.

I write for those who may feel disconnected, burdened by life's hardships, or trapped in a cycle of doubt and despair. It is to them I wish to convey a simple but powerful message: You are not alone. No matter how isolating the current moment may seem, there exists a future where light and clarity await. Somewhere beyond the horizon of your current vision, there is a place of hope, happiness, and peace. This place may not be visible now, and the path toward it may feel obscured, but it is real and attainable. It is a destination reached not just by the passage of time but by the healing power of forgiveness.

Forgiveness, as I explore within these pages, is not solely about absolving others who may have wronged us. More critically, it is about learning to forgive ourselves. Too often, we carry the weight of our mistakes, regrets, or perceived failures like a burden that grows heavier with time. But true healing begins when we can release that burden, recognize our intrinsic worth, and allow ourselves the grace to be human, imperfect, and evolving.

It is my sincere hope that through the stories, reflections, and lessons shared in this work, readers will find solace in knowing that their struggles are part of the shared human experience. And in those moments of deep reflection, they might catch a glimpse of that distant place where forgiveness – both from others and from themselves – paves the way to a brighter, more hopeful tomorrow.

MARKS OF LOVE

Love From A Distance

In the quiet hush of the night's embrace,
I picture her in soft moonlight's grace.
So petite and lithe, with curves so alluring and fine,
Perfect in every way, oh how I wish she was mine.

For me she is a goddess born from silk and flame,
When she walks, the world around her she does tame.
In her eyes I see ponds of deep and filled with wild desire,
They spark within thoughts that burn and inspire.

Her wry smile, like a secret with which she does tease,
A subtle power that so easily brings me to my knees.
Her presence lingers long in my mind, so soft yet so bold,
Such beauty and grace I find so rare, a story untold.

Though I believe that I will never hold her close,
Images of her beauty continue to haunt me, like a ghost.
In dreams, she dances with me through my mind,
A vision so alluring, lips so warm, and so perfectly kind.

She's the kind of beauty that I'll never claim,
But still, in my mind she will burn in private flame.
And in the silence of my dreams, I will always see,
This beautiful woman, whom I feel will never be with me.

The Welcoming

Display your light, and shine it bright my beautiful child,
It matters not in life if you are placid or wild,

Whether you walk the road amongst all the others,
Or walk on a mere track, to leave your sisters and brothers,

We are all unique, and this I tell you this my beautiful one,
Walk your journey confidently, and be proud when it is done,

For in life your walk, will be mostly alone despite what they say,
Along a journey filled with wonder and hardship each day,

But listen closely to the wind and then you may just hear,
My cries of support blowing softly through your ear,

For though you may not always see me standing there,
In my heart you shall always live, and I will always care,

And when the day comes that you reach the end of your trek,
You will see me there triumphantly waiting for you to welcome you back.

The Guardian Angel

Have you ever heard the dark voices call,
Or battled hard to keep on standing tall,

Felt the darkest depths of sheer despair,
Believed that no one could still really care,

Looked to the future but saw only black,
Whilst life seems to send constant waves of attack,

Maybe you stumbled, tripped and then fell,
But not one person heard you cry or yell,

Have the lights gone off that lit your world,
Whilst into the darkness you were hurled,

Were the walls too steep to climb back once more,
So now you lay there, bruised, battered and sore,

Please take my hand, and let me be your guide,
From me you truly have nothing to hide,

Let me tend your wounds, and keep you warm,
Till once more you regain your normal form,

Let me support you whilst I draw you near,
Dispelling those things which you so fear,

My child I love you and will always be there,
To guide and protect you and always care,

So stand tall and let me be strong for you,
And guide you to live your life with courage anew.

A Poem For Ruby

*Eighteen years of age, it's a golden dawn,
Your world awaits, your path is drawn,
But tread with care, and mind your heart,
For life's a journey, not just a start,*

*Dream your dreams, and dream them bold,
But beware, for not all roads are paved with gold,
Some paths will twist, and some may bend,
Yet every step you take, will help you ascend,*

*Listen well, and trust your inner voice,
Your instincts will be there to guide your choice,
Kindness and strength - they both can blend,
In giving, you'll receive back my friend,*

*Know your worth, and never shrink,
You're stronger than you sometimes think,
In love, be brave, but guard your soul,
For self-love too, will make you whole,*

*Don't fear the falls, for again you'll rise,
Each stumble a lesson that makes you wise,
For every fall you always rise, and when you do,
The world will again be your grand debut,*

*Remember that time will always flow,
So cherish all moments as they grow,
You're eighteen now, but it's only the start,
So go light the world and fulfill your heart.*

A Toast to Life

*As I look back upon my life, not with sadness but with joy,
Standing now as a man, but from once was a boy,*

*I smile when I think of old friends and of foe,
Or lessons I learnt as through life I did go,*

*Of money that passed through hand, in trickle or flood,
Spent well with those who were of friend or of blood,*

*Times spent sober, and times spent quite drunk,
Washed and showered, or smelling worse than a skunk,*

*Of times of agape love, and times of great pain,
Though every time was a lesson from which I would gain,*

*Times bonding with friends, or fighting with foe,
Though this journey of life, I have never been afraid to go,*

*Looking back, I admit that in my life, my proudest call,
Was fatherhood, and my sons three were my greatest gift of all,*

*So I lift my glass and say thank you to all whom I have known,
And ahead on this journey, on which we have all travelled and grown,*

*May there still always be good times ahead that we can share,
For in my heart, for all of you, whether friend or foe, I will always care.*

Time

Time and love go by and never stop to sleep,
They give us so many beautiful memories to keep,

Some bring happiness and some bring pain,
But in the end, they're all the same,

They help us learn and they help us grow,
We pass these lessons on to others to show,

How love often offers us the time to heal,
The time to love and the time to feel,

Time and love are infinite, but our lives here are not,
So, cherish the time here for we don't get a lot,

Please love one another and show them in kind,
And look for the good in others and do not be blind,

Love is just like time and eternal you see,
And does not grow old and die like you or me,

There will be some in your life who will do you wrong,
But forgive them in kind and then send them on,

Try not to harbour any hate in your heart and let love your anger tame,
Grant time permission to heal and allow love to ease your pain,

So, enjoy this day, and remember it could always be worse,
And whether you listen and take heed now of my little verse,

It will not matter to me for I am merely planting the seed,
That one day may flower for you to show others to take heed,

And the beauty that once was planted that is now in full flower,
So others may hopefully realize that love is truly the greatest power.

Chain-Smoking Memories

The peace and solitude of quiet outdoors I sought,
trying to calm a troubling thought,
One that weighed heavy on my heart and mind,
and peace and quiet I dearly sought,

Whilst there I grabbed a pack of memories,
and held them in my mind,
Memories of all my days gone by,
that were now left far behind,

One by one I chain-smoked them all,
without a break between,
While visions of both good times
and bad were now so clearly seen,

I saw all my ups and downs,
and compared them to my present,
And understood that all these things,
were all merely lessons sent,

That each of them I had enjoyed, learnt from,
or conquered in the past,
And that times of either good or bad,
none are ever sent to last,

So, with a clearer mind I stood,
and I stride ahead to meet my new fate,
New lessons are there waiting to greet me,
and nothing I do will make them wait,

*So, I stand up straight, and boldly go forth armed
with knowledge, love, faith, and hope,*

*For with these tools in my heart, my mind,
and my soul, I will always carry the courage to cope.*

The Promise

Sinister thoughts swim and fill your mind,
Evil thoughts that surround you so unkind,

Crippling fear, tears at you, tugging at you,
Pulling you along like you're stuck with glue,

Scenes of fear and guilt come to the fore,
While your sanity it falls, heavy thud to the floor,

Your eyes are wide, though see, they do not,
Your strength is gone, and return it will not,

Do you hear the screams call you in the night,
That tainted scream, so filled with fright,

Let them all go my dearest friend,
And I will stay with you to the end,

I know that you will question the truth,
But for now, I cannot show you any proof,

Trust that our bond together will never end,
And in the afterlife your soul I will mend.

A Poem for Penny

Penny, the battle you fought was one that was long and hard, but you stoically faced it true and strong,

We stood by your side and offered support, but our lives collapsed the day we realized, that soon you'd be gone,

For 21 years we watched as you fought one heck of a battle, bravely facing your fears, and never once did you cower,

Truly a beacon of light to many, you became their symbol of hope, and in many eyes, a strong and mighty tower,

Your husband, and your two wonderful sons, they'll all continue to love you and hold you close in their heart and soul,

For they lost a loving wife and mother, and left behind what can only be described as an unfathomable hole,

Penny your family, and your parents, who also feel the indescribable pain of your loss, along with the friends that you knew,

All of them will miss you and everyone's mind will ask the same question, "Penny, why was it you?"

But despite your passing, you have taught all of us so much in your short time, while here on Earth,

Giving us all so many memories and sharing so much love and guidance that will always be priceless in worth,

Each of us here have received from Penny the seeds of courage and love, that in our hearts she did sow,

And in our hearts, they have taken root, and despite Penny's passing, they all will continue to grow,

For unlike our lives, this valuable gift that she left us is certainly not finite, and will surely never end,

So please cultivate the beauty she left in your heart and receive with thanks the gifts she continues to send.

My Plea

So lonely are those that in society feel they cannot fit in,
Reaching out from their holes they are hidden well within,

They watch others as though through windows from a room,
Knowing that they cannot join, and so sit in their own gloom,

The barriers before them are not imaginary for them you see,
They are solid and real and from their walls they cannot flee,

Many choose to look upon them with disdain, disgust, and hate,
When what we should all be doing, is helping them to integrate,

So quick are we to help someone injured and bloody that we find,
Yet those who are injured in psyche, we all just tend to leave behind,

A kind word now and then, a helping hand, to held out in kind,
Can go a long way to start the healing process of their troubled mind,

Sometimes we can all lose our way, as we travel along our road,
When our journey gets rough sometimes, we carry an enormous load,

So, if it's no problem, can I ask of you all in this coming year,
Do not just walk past, when you see someone looking in fear,

When you see someone struggling, or with a tear in their eye,
Look at them and say hello, ask, are you ok? and at least try,

To break down the terrible barriers that our eyes cannot see,
But are so real to these people...I know...for that person was once me.

The Decision

The road of life lies ahead, and I can never see far for it seems to always end,
Falling away to the horizon, or in my path another obstacle, or awkward bend,

There are times when you can see off to the distance for quite a way,
Yet other times you struggle to see clearly, even in the bright light of a clear day,

Then up ahead the road will change once more and deteriorates yet again,
From smooth roads and freeways to dirt road and potholes that can cause you great pain,

But up ahead I see a fork in the road, one is smooth and offers a more comfortable ride,
The other less travelled, strewn with rocks and obstacles, and now I must decide,

Which path will I travel on this next journey in my life, which decision will I make?
The smooth road this time or the difficult and rough, which path do I take?

Shall I take what is easy this time and follow the crowd, or shall I do what is right?
To follow the masses and go with the flow, or leave them and do for me what is right?

In my mirror I look, and I can see all the way back to my journey's start,
Now I look down the road and decide... I will follow the map in my heart.

Connections

Through the flashes and pictures in my mind I see,
The beautiful young girl that once lived next door to me,

Captivating and cheeky she has such a beautiful smile,
There were times she would come over and talk for a while,

But she was too young for me then, so everyone said,
Warning me to dispel any thoughts of her from my head,

Yet today here we are 40 years on, and time equals us all,
Last night I rang you and we spoke for hours during this call,

You spoke of many things and of the times you had,
But deep down within you I heard something that made me quite sad,

A sadness or pain you were trying to hide from the world,
But as we spoke last night, like a flower you unfurled,

Your voice still so familiar, your beauty has not waned,
Though my size has increased as weight I have gained,

But now I look forward to Friday when again we will meet,
Taking you out for an Italian meal the night will be a real treat,

So, till then my dearest friend may I say thank you for reconnecting and I pray,
That whatever sadness is in your life, in time my love for you will chase away.

My Wonderful Sons

Three sons have I and I love them all,
Though one passed over when God did call,

I have watched you other two grow with pride,
Together we took life's hard knocks in our stride,

Dane and Scott, I love you dearly guys,
Along with Kyle you're the sparkle in my eyes,

So please never doubt the way I feel,
For if I am the yacht then you are my keel,

You kept me upright as we battled wild seas,
And in calmer weather we would do as we please,

A team of battlers a team bound by love,
We may be fingers alone but we wear the same glove,

Working as a team, we've hit some home runs,
And I couldn't be prouder of my wonderful sons.

When Words Fall Short

How do I find the words to say to you what I truly feel,
When the words "thank you" seem too small, too unreal?

For the hands that lifted me when I was weak,
And the hearts that heard me when I couldn't speak.

You stood like pillars beside me, steadfast and true,
Through the dark when I stumbled, you helped me through.

Not with grand gestures, no, there was no grandstanding at all,
Just your quiet presence you gave to me, ...this gift said it all.

The simple phrase, "Thank you", feels hollow and slight,
To match the belief in me that you showed with your guiding light.

How can mere words strung together ever convey,
The weight of gratitude that I feel for you each day?

For me it is far more than words, this bond we share,
It's a tapestry woven with respect, love and care.

In each thread there is kindness, a moment, a gift,
Like a ships' steadying anchor, or a soul's gentle lift.

So please hear me now, though my words still may lack,
My heart overflows because of you, and there's no holding back.

For all the kindness you've given, for all that you still do,
Know that this world is far brighter place... because of you.

Friends

There was a young lady who lacked some height,
Others would think it was a terrible plight,

But not this young woman as courage she'd pluck,
To tell us all she didn't give a fuck,

Bold and brassy you spoke your mind,
Though in your heart you were always kind,

In stitches she had us as she told her tale,
This young woman that we called "Little Gail",

Now it's lovely to see that she is still the same,
And even father time still cannot tame,

The fire in her belly and love in her heart,
As friendship again we pick up to start,

Thank you, Gail, for memories of a great time,
And for reconnecting now in our prime,

In Lillian's heart I know you still live,
And together kindness and love you will give,

And one day I would love to join you both and catch up,
For us to all catch up and drink deep from life's' cup,

Mama

Mama, you were always there for me,
to help me up when I fell,
When I was scared or feeling blue you could always tell,

There were times when I was small,
when the path got rough you held my hand,
Then times I needed someone to talk to,
and you would always understand,

When I cried you were there to wipe the rears
away from my cheek,
And you were there to give me strength when
I was feeling weak,

You watched, and tried to guide me as
I grew into a young man,
And watched on with concern when
I bought my first panel van,

You were there when I married and
you were so proud of me,
And looked on so lovingly as children I had three,

You cried with me when my second son,
Kyle, passed away,
Later as my marriage broke down you gave me
and the boys a safe place to stay,

You always supported me Mama and I still love you so,
Your son once a baby, then a boy, into a fine man did grow,

*But this would not have been possible if not
for the love that you gave,*
*And the lessons in life you imparted, about love,
wisdom and how to behave!*

*Not a day goes by when I don't think of you Mama,
and I love you still,*
*And here in a special part of my heart you live,
and Mama, you always will.*

Self-made - For Lexi

Beneath the sun's first golden light,
A woman stands, her spirit bright.

Her eyes reflect the storms she's faced,
Each trial is carved, no dream erased.

No silver path, no gilded crown,
Her worth was built from falling down.

Brick by brick, through sweat and flame,
She rose and claimed the "Self-made" name.

Her shoulders square, proud head held high,
A phoenix born to kiss the sky.

Though whispers seek to dull her fire,
She turned to ash each false desire.

The world threw chains, but she broke free,
Forging strength from adversity.

Her hands may ache, her heart may tire,
But still she climbs, her eyes inspire.

For every scar that she wears with grace,
Tell of her battles that none could erase.

Her triumphs hum a fierce refrain
"I fought, I bled, but I'll rise again."

*Confidently she walks where dreams reside,
Unyielding, bold, and dignified.*

*Her name a banner, so proudly displayed
A legacy forever, her title – Self-made.*

A Poem for Barbara

*A wonderful woman of Irish decent that I know,
A beautiful woman whom I adore and love so,*

*A true and loyal friend is she and we go back some time,
When we were working together and both in our prime,*

*She has a soul filled with love and a heart made of gold,
When this woman was created, they surely broke the mould,*

*For I truly believe God was showing off on that day,
When He created Barbara in such a beautiful way,*

*She's a loyal friend that gives without expectation,
Who I dare say is as fiercely protective as a loyal Alsatian,*

*And I thank the Lord that when my time comes to an end,
I can look back on my life richer, for having her as a friend,*

*Barbara thank you for sharing parts of your path with me here,
For these are moments I shall always hold incredibly dear,*

*Though different shoes we may have been wearing,
Our friendship was built on honesty, sharing and caring.*

The New Morning

*When the sun begins to set and darkness rolls in,
It brings with it sorrow as fear and sadness begin,*

*All those who stand, and watch are smitten with grief and pain,
Whilst those that enter the darkness will end their life's reign,*

*Yet this darkness is like night and will eventually give way,
With a new brilliant sunrise to start their new day,*

*So, whilst we may grieve while watching this on us beset,
For her comes new life to follow this final sunset,*

*Words of love we have all spoken as you head toward your new start,
As we tearfully farewell to you on your journey with love and sorrow in our heart,*

*Sail on my sweet loving mother whom we all love so and adore,
And thank you for the memories we will hold in our hearts and cherish for evermore.*

My Love, My Soul Mate, My Destiny

I often still think back and recall the first time we talked
and how you so coyly said Hi,
How red you went as you struggled to talk to me,
and I could not understand why,

Remembering the times that followed when we would talk
and how I fell in love with you,
The times we would just spend, lost in each other's
presence, and yet I never saw or knew,

How much you really thought of me, or the depth of love
for me that you held in your heart,
Unfortunately, there were others who held a different view,
working hard to keep us apart,

Though you were young I genuinely loved you, but then life
took us on a different turn,
And I never saw you again for years, though my love for
you always continued to burn,

Came the fateful day our paths did cross once more,
and love for you I could finally show,
But it was not to last, and life again stepped in to stop our
love, and again I had to go,

I always thought of you, holding you in my heart,
reminiscing of that fateful day you said Hi,
And I hoped and prayed we would meet again, so I could
tell you why I never said goodbye,

For goodbye is far too final, and I knew that for you my heart would always wait,

If I died while waiting here on Earth, I would continue my vigil to greet you at heaven's gate,

Now my prayers are answered, and we are now as one, with my life full of only love for you,

I promise never to leave you again my love, and will forever shower you with love so true,

For despite the meddling of others, what always should have been, has finally come to be,

And the depth of love we have for each other, is now so plain for all around us to see.

The Brave Survivor - A Poem for Tracey

Abused and tortured in your youth, causing so much confusion,
Life has flooded you with lessons, that almost drowned you with its profusion,

A tumultuous time filled with so much sorrow and pain,
Your world filled with hurt as others used and abused you for their gain,

So many people that took advantage of your good-natured being,
Never seeing the beautiful side of you that in your mind was sent fleeing,

The scars that they left, unlike physical ones, are not visible to all,
For they are all hidden inside, deep behind an almost impenetrable wall,

One that you built to help you cope with life's cruelty and strife,
Made not of bricks or mortar, but from the very torments of life,

Then life served you with health issues, mixed with indescribable pain,
Things that would send those not as strong as you, irreversibly insane,

But through all of the challenges that life at you has thrown,
It has created in you an amazing and resilient woman, that within you has grown,

Whilst there are times, I know when you feel like you are drowning inside,
Your spiritual strength and determination to get through does not hide,

It wields not a sword to maim others or kill, but a feather of love and of grace,
Defending you, healing you and confronting your issues head on, face to face,

Through this you have learnt wisdom, understanding, love and forgiveness,
Enabling you now to carry staunchly on with life's everyday business,

You prominently stand out amongst others as the true bearer of light,
A signal of strength for all you meet to never give up on their fight,

There are those that love you, and are very proud of you too,
And I count Debbie and myself amongst the many that do.

We love you, Tracey.

Just Till the Morning

Laying here I slowly close my eyes, as the dusk falls on my life,
All pain and worry have left me, as I leave this world of strife,

Your sorrow pains me to see, and I try to hang on one more day,
But my time here has reached its end, and we struggle what to say,

Then the words just seem to come to me, and I take you by the hand,
Uttering the words I feel and believe, and hope you understand,

This is not farewell or goodbye my love, only time for me to sleep,
So, till the morning I'll wait for you to join me, my love please do not weep,

So let me say goodnight for now, and in the morning, we will again be as one,
To start our new chapter of love together, that will shine as bright and radiant as the sun.

My Promise To You

Gently I kiss you with my lips to yours, so soft to touch,
Fingertips lightly caressing your skin, sometimes the electricity too much,

I look deep in your eyes and see the frailties you hide,
Touch the scars from the others, and feel the many times that you cried,

I wrap you in arms that hold you close to my heart,
And whisper to you that this time, we'll never again part,

For my love for you runs so deep and runs so long,
My heart beating only for you, playing true love's song,

Rest now in my arms my sweetest darling, and when you awake,
The gift of my heart, my soul, my all, I lay before you to take.

MOMENTS OF TRANSCENDENCE

The Beauty of a Woman

*She walks with grace, like a gentle breeze,
A light that shines through life's stormy seas.*

*Her smile, though bright, is merely the start,
For the real beauty lies within her heart.*

*Her kindness and caring, so soft, can heal your soul,
With a loving that makes others feel whole.*

*In every word, you'll find warmth and care,
From her quiet strength that is beyond compare.*

*Her hands are soft, yet strong they still be,
And they help guide those too tired to see.*

*She carries much love, and to all it shows,
A beauty true, that the heart just knows.*

*Her mind is sharp and her spirit free,
She's a dreamer with a fierce loyalty.*

*She sees the good even when others fall,
And finds a way to rise through it all.*

*Her beauty isn't just confined to the skin,
But in the place where all dreams begin.*

*For it's her soul that so brightly does glow,
With a light that every heart should know.*

Not just in her face or body, but in every part,
She holds those she loves cupped within her heart.

For in her eyes, the truth is always crystal clear,
And her beauty only grows with every year.

Nightly Reunion

*Dancing in the moonlight, to the music carried on the wind,
I feel the earth beneath our feet alive and in the moment,
Watching the air itself electric and sparking to the tune,
And the clouds booming in time to keep the beat,*

*Lights flash across the sky as once again we embrace,
My eyes locked on the sparkling beauty that is yours,
Hands trembling as they touch your velvet soft skin,
Your lips touch mine and the ice on my heart melts again,*

*You smile and your love fills the gaping maul in my chest,
Morning breaks and once again I stir from dreams,
Breaking light chases the dark and washes your image away,
Alone I lay again with my heart heavy and broken,*

*Yet your memory dances so beautifully still in my mind,
The day I lost you was the day my world collapsed,
It is my heart only that keeps the memory of you alive,
And your memory that alive my heart keeps and in turn, me.*

*Tonight, I slumber and will again meet you in my dreams,
And there once more my heart with beat with lively rhythm,
Till the day I too will remain in sleep eternal and find peace,
For there we will forever be together, and I will always love you.*

The Ocean

By the shore of ocean great I stand,
With peaceful mind and outstretched hand,

Calling out to the mother sea,
Thanking her for birthing me,

The smell of salt it fills the air,
For in my mind is not a care,

Greatest love I feel for this great body of water,
Stronger than the bond between bricks and mortar,

She offers food me with her bountiful feast,
And in her swims Earth's largest beast,

Any stress or pains, she will wash away,
And rejuvenate you in every way,

She'll feed you, calm you and keep you fit,
Washing and caressing you whilst in waves you flit,

What greater love is there that you can conceive,
Than the ocean's love for us that we all can receive.

Free

Loving you wasn't easy,
You were always so unkind,
Loving you wasn't easy,
I almost lost my mind,

But now I'm free,
Free to be me,
Yes now I'm free,
Free to be me,

You treated me so bad girl,
Lying to me all the time,
Cheated with my best friend,
Was being faithful such a crime,

But now I'm free,
Free to be me,
Yes, now I'm free,
Free to be me,

You sent me out of my mind,
You drove me of to hell,
You left me in the gutter,
You destroyed me so well,

But now I'm free,
Free to be me,
Yes, now I'm free,
Free to be me,

*You walked away and left me,
You took my friends as well,
But I've since gotten better,
And baby, all I shall tell,*

*That I'm now free
Free to be me,
Yes, now I'm free,
Free to be me,*

*Baby I'm now flying,
Soaring through the sky
Don't need drugs to fuel me,
Cause I'm on a natural high,*

*And now I'm free,
Free to be me,
Yes, now I'm free,
Free to be me,*

*For now, I'm free,
Free to be me,
Yes, now I'm free,
Free to be me.*

The Touch of Music

Do not believe the words of doubt that scream and thunder in your head,
Take my advice, cast them aside, and listen to music instead,

Swim in pools of music that touch your soul creating love and tranquillity,
Engulf yourself in music that frees your mind to sail, like a yacht upon the sea,

Music has the power to heal, allow the tunes of music to heal your soul,
It calms the savage beast they say, and I believe it will again make you whole,

Start each and every day with song to lift your soul to the greatest height,
And end each day with music to help you gently unwind and rest to greet the night.

A Gift of Sight Beyond

I heard a noise at twilight's door and answered it to see,
An angel of true beauty standing there and beckoning to me,

Her hair was burning red, and eyes were lit like burning star,
She beckoned me come and see the alternate world in another dimension so far,

To see what others do not see and broaden my earthly mind,
For opening this could help me with true wisdom, further, to find,

I saw the many that had passed and the many travelled on,
But some remained to stay behind, their direction lost and gone,

Then she elevated me to heights so high, and gently set me down again,
Amongst the people that I know and other worlds that began to wane,

Occasionally I see her still, and this other world I still long to explore,
And I'll not forget the moment I found an angel standing at my door.

Pavlova

Whilst enjoying my favourite dessert last night there occurred to me a thought,
This dessert that I was enjoying so much, was filling my head with fraught,

For before me was not just a dessert, itself so tasty and perfect in every way,
But the personification of the perfect woman was sitting before me this day,

To look at she is beautiful, with loads of tempting fruit and sweetness that she adorns,
And there covering her is an outer crust, which whilst still sweet, it warns you of her horns,

Tempting peaches, melons, or cherries, adding curves draped in silky, smoothest cream,
Causing wonder for those caught in her spell, of the tastes of her passionfruit to dream,

Around the base there lies her shell to protect her from any unwanted blow,
Yet beneath this thin veil of protective armour, is a treat that only a select few will know,

And if you are lucky enough that she allows you to taste, or enter deep inside,
There you will find a velvety soft sweetness, that from others she does hide,

*Yes, here before me is the epitome of the perfect woman,
and I savour every taste,*

*Relishing every morsel, as I deliver them with anticipation
to my mouth, slowly and without hurry, speed, or haste.*

My Plight

I thought I would go to the beach today and catch myself some sun,
But I was surely surprised when around me hordes of people did soon come,

Now I know I am overweight, and could stand to lose some fat,
But covering me in wet towels and keeping me wet, now really, where is that at?

I tried to protest, I really tried, but the soft sand made it difficult to stand,
Meanwhile they are all screaming, "This animal shouldn't be on land!"

Then around me someone tied some ropes, and they towed me out to sea,
My God this day is getting worse, while they are all screaming with glee,

They cut me lose about 2 kilometres out to sea and so my next challenge does begin,
I looked back at the distant shoreline, and started back on my long swim,

I finally reached the shore that evening, and made my way back home,
Just in time to see myself on the news, a video saving a beached whale was shown,

That night I made my mind up and started my new diet, now soon I'll be slim and trim,

I've even got a personal trainer, and taken a 12-month membership at the local gym,

They will not let me do push-ups yet; afraid that I'll change Earth's orbit around the sun,
And they are far too scared to let me use the treadmill to attempt a little run,

And all this distancing from others during Covid is a little hard for me,
As my body is so large that like a planet I create my own gravity,

NASA once tracked me for days thinking they found another star,
They were very disappointed when they tracked me to a snack bar,

But this problem is about to go and soon they will not mistake me for a whale,
And I can live a normal life again, to end this sorrowful tale.

The Meeting Place

Where the roads to our final judgements end, and meets with the garden where new life does begin,

There, you will find that the preconceived ideas of right and wrong are dispelled and here no longer exist,

Come and meet there and I will rest with you amongst the beauty of the trees and gardens of beauty and love,

Let us come to understand and accept each other and build on our similarities and not dispute our differences,

Together we can plant new life and give up our judgements and embrace the newfound love that surrounds us all.

The Encounter

Somewhere in our conversation the words you spoke touched my heart and soul on that fateful night,

Almost as though you travelled to the darkest corners of my very existence, and there reaching in, you switched on the light,

Though you did not stay for long, I am forever indebted to your simple act of pure love and kind,

And I often return to that fateful night when I revisit the corridors filled with memories and lessons you planted in my mind.

Going Home

In twilight's hush her husband sighs,
His body weary from being beneath today's skies,

He sinks into his chair's comforting embrace,
As shadows begin to dance upon his face,

Flashes come to him in a vivid stream,
Of battles fought and dreams that gleam,

He sees the roads, both rough and wide,
Of laughter shared, of tears he cried,

Childhood's laughter, love's sweet call,
The weight of loss, he felt them all,

Each moment coloured in both dark and light,
Like a tapestry woven of day and night,

He feels the struggle of the burdened years,
The silent hopes and whispered fears,

Yet through each storm the sun would break,
In every heartache some joy would wake,

But suddenly a light, so pure, so clear,
Draws him closer erasing all his fear,

He stands unbound in its soft embrace,
No longer held by feelings of time or space,

A breath of peace comes then euphoria's grace,
No pain remains now, just endless space,

He smiles, remembering all he's left behind,
A journey full and proud, his heart is aligned,

In that bright light he finds peace and rest,
The feeling of euphoria and love, he feels truly blessed,

No shadows linger now, no tears are here to find,
He's home at last, for in this light he is now unconfined.

Back in the early 1980s I was called to a house. The fellow who lived there had just come home and lovingly greeted his wife and told her that he was feeling tired and asked her for a cup of tea. His wife left the room to go to the kitchen to boil the kettle and upon her return she found that he had passed away on his chair. She was obviously quite distraught, yet when I looked at him, he was sitting there peacefully with almost a smile on his face. It was a surreal experience for me seeing him in such peace, and yet I felt great sorrow and empathy for his wife.

This poem is dedicated to that man and the lasting impression he left on me.

Sweet Sounds

Voice like treacle smooth and thick,
She sings with grace while guitar that he will pick,

Talented two with presence and flare,
They play with such passion as their gift they share,

Let them take you on a journey so surreal,
Your mind transported new experience to feel,

They'll dive in and touch your heart and your soul,
Removing the burden of life's heavy toll,

Together they play and connect as one,
Sara in song and whilst he does strum,

Memories of life they bring to the fore,
Of good time and hard times, I have known before,

Photos in my mind that become so clear,
Memories that sometimes creep from my eye as a tear,

But mostly I sit transported, my face locked in smile,
As I am taken on a journey of beauty for a while,

I look at them both and see in their eyes,
Respect and love for each other they cannot disguise,

Their souls intertwined by music and love of their gift,
I listen to them play... and slowly away I will drift.

A Poem For Afia

*From magical and mystical lands so far away
She flew on clouds of angel dust they say,*

*Like a princess adorned in rivers of gold,
She ages not, yet rumoured to be over 500 years old,*

*Her sparkling eyes light the darkest night,
Whilst her golden skin is such a delight,*

*Her voice will caress your ears with its words so soft,
One look from her will surely send you aloft,*

*With gentle spirit but with a fiery heart,
She shares both worlds so far apart,*

*Like treacle pouring so tempting and sweet,
She's a delight to know should you chance to meet,*

*Her smile extends so wide, it seems to have no end,
Afia I am proud to call you, "My Mystic Friend".*

The Healer

Within you, a long way down and deep inside,
Therein dwells the feelings that you try to hide,

You struggle to hide them all from the world,
Whilst the child deep within lies there curled,

You dare not speak and tell anyone,
That your mind is lost and you're feeling numb,

Yet you feel that this one person is true,
That if you talk, he is one who will not betray you,

You start in short sentences, one at a time,
Things you still hide, almost like they're a crime,

He judges not, but does merely sits and does listen,
You begin realising there is no danger in his position,

Slowly you begin to open more of yourself,
And he listens, in turn he tells you some of himself,

The weight is lifting and setting you free,
Your eyes start to glisten, and you begin to see,

The world does show caring, love and peace,
You slowly begin to feel a whole new lease,

He is a healer of souls, a carer, a giver of love,
And he will restart your heart with a velvet glove,

He belongs to no one and one day may go,
But he will plant the seed, in you to grow,

And in your heart, it will grow and belong,
For the world will soon see a new you, now strong.

The River

I dreamed of a river that flowed through my soul, a stream of time, gentle and whole.
Above, I floated, weightless and free, watching myself in the river's decree.

There I stood, in waters so clear, a younger version of me, unburdened by fear.
The river whispered, its voice soft and low, carrying all the moments where memories grow.

Each ripple bore fragments of my youth, stories of wonder, sadness, laughter, and truth.
As they drifted downstream, I watched them depart, pieces of joy and ache from my heart.

New memories formed like petals in bloom, swept by the river to their watery tomb.
Yet the ocean awaited, eternal and vast, a sanctuary where all moments amassed.

Then I saw myself, aged and grey, lying in the current at the end of my stay.
The river embraced me, tender and wise, carrying me toward the ocean's sunrise.

I stood where I had once been before, but the memories, now shadows, returned no more.
Their essence lingered, like whispers in air, yet the flow of the river left nothing there.

For such is the river, relentless and true, it takes what is old and welcomes the new.

You may revisit, reflect, and also recall, but to relive the past will bring on your fall.

For the river of life flows steady and deep, a home of memories which we cannot keep.

And it delivers us eventually to the sea, to a place of great beauty and peace, in eternity.

A Daughter's Love

The love that is shared between a father and daughter is one of the strongest loves we know,
Protecting her and guiding her as the love between them over time does grow,

From the time she is just a little babe, his love on her he'll pour, and a special bond they'll share,
From a little graze on the knee, to her first relationship breakup, her father is always there,

He gives her away when she is wed, and continues to shower love on her when she becomes a bit wild,
She calls on him when times are tough and shares with him when she is pregnant with child,

But father time moves on and never stops, and this life we are gifted is not ours to keep,
Time takes with him her father's youth and his health and then helps him cross to eternal sleep,

Even then, during this time of illness when a daughter's world turns inside out and the pain seems to last forever,
The bond between them grows even stronger as they share special times together,

And when that fateful day that looms does come and he moves on to another plane,
Her world will change so suddenly, and unfortunately, will never be the same,

But the love they had for each other will in fact last forever and his love she will always feel,

For while they sailed on the sea of life, he was and will always be with her, as her steadying keel.

For My Love

*Across a timeless ocean,
I sail this ship alone,
My destination ahead I see,
It is there I will see her waiting,
To reunite with once again,
And as I pull into the pier,
Her face lights up with love,
She climbs on board to join me,
And we sail off together once more,
But now time does not concern us,
Not age nor old and weary bone,
Our love will light and guide our way forward,
As together we will sail forever more.*

For a Great Woman

*An angel fallen from the heavens so high,
When she left, she surely left the Gods to cry,*

*What a loss she was to her heavenly home,
Just so that upon this she could Earth roam,*

*Then she met the man that would change her life,
He loved her so and would take her for his wife,*

*His name was Peter, and he charmed her so,
That the love between them like a river did flow,*

*He courted her lovingly, and stayed by her side,
Then came the day she became his heavenly bride,*

*But still not content as an angel Earthward sent,
She showed her talent for baking, oh what a heavenly scent,*

*First came cakes, so delightfully tasting and wickedly sweet,
Followed by pastries and toppings on cakes, oh what a treat,*

*And not only did she continue to cook with pleasant surprise,
But as she got older, she became more beautiful in his eyes,
Occasionally the heavens will still visit her, burning so bright,
To place a large order to cater for all the other angels of light,*

*They decided never to replace her in that heavenly place,
And there still sits her chair, always empty, waiting, just in case.*

Love Complete

You listen to your heart and feel it beating quickly as you lay there in dim light,
Feeling it pounding harder with love and lust as it builds your sexual appetite,

There is the scent of rose petals that are scattered across the bed everywhere,
Scented candles burn also, sending their perfumed aroma mixing with cool night air,
Music plays softly and French champagne sparkles and flows freely without care,

Wrapped in silken sheets you're still wet from the shower that you both shared,
He slides in bed beside you, your mind racing, for you know you are about to be paired,

Tonight, you'll give your body freely in pleasure and love, and yet, you still start to blush,
Your lips slowly touch as his hands touch your body, and you feel your blood rush,

He starts slowly, a massage and warm oil, time is of no issue, he's removing all worry,
Pouring warm scented oil over your body his fingers slowly explore, for he's in no hurry,

The scent of the roses fills the air, and you feel your senses begin to heighten and peak,
When his firm masculine hands run over your body and while every square inch to seek,

He gives pleasure you so eagerly deserve while entering the zone of your heavenly urge,
Then his tongue explores every inch of your womanly body as your two bodies merge,

The tempo of music seems to pulse in time, ever increasing as your rhythm increases,
You both move from place to place both trying different positions, different creases.

Time flows slowly like honey, but you feel the time is coming when you both will erupt.
Deep inside of you from behind, trembling with pleasure, your breasts he holds cupped.

Electricity bolts through your body as you both peak in time, collapsing, both spent.
He holds close, you're feeling loved and safe, breathing deeply, he looks into your eyes.
You see a soft smile and true love in his eyes that he does not try to hide or disguise.

Laying there spent and exhausted, but left feeling like you're floating on heavenly highs,
But the night's not over, and he starts once more, and you softly moan as he caresses your thighs.

Whispering Dreams

Dedicated to and written for Jenny

In a quiet room where shadows flicker and play,
A young woman drifts through the end of a day,

Her face, like dawn, in the soft light glows,
However, her heart is bound where ink on paper flows,

Pages flutter like soft whispering dreams,
In the hush of a world where her imagination streams,

She reads of new realms dark, exotic and bright,
As her day begins to blend seamlessly into night,

Her eyes, like dark wells filled with stories deep,
Dive into new worlds where echoes sleep,

Each line a doorway and each paragraph a gate,
Taking her to lands where destiny, dreams, and magic await,

Her fingers trace across the written lore,
Each touch and line the key to a brand-new door,

She dances through tales of pain, courage, love and grace,
Finding solace in each verse of fictive embrace,

The world outside is now merely a distant drone,
Here in the realm of words, she is always free to come home,

Through the labyrinth of letters there she does roam,
Crafting a sanctuary where she builds her dream home,

Lost in the pages, her worries diminish and fade,
In this tapestry of dreams, she's now unafraid,

Her soul finds wings where the words take flight,
In the boundless expanse of this written night,

And as time weaves on with its quiet thread,
She sees the evening wane and shadows spread,

But in her silent retreat, she's there to be found,
To the echoes of stories where her heart is unbound,

Beautiful and young, with a heart free and wide,
She lives in the stories, where her spirit is free to glide,

In the written word she may be lost, yet there she is free,
Finding herself sailing in these stories on her own endless sea.

An Evening of Love

Beneath the soft glow of the evening's embrace,
He stands with her in sanctuary, her solace, her grace,

With hands skilled in comfort, tender and true,
He whispers through his touch, "This is all just for you."

His fingers weave magic, each stroke a caress,
Easing her tension, her worry, her stress,

She melts in his hands, a soft sigh on her lips,
As he kneads away burdens from her shoulders to hips,

The bath now is drawn, warm waters that steam,
Scented with lavender, perfumed like a sweet dream,

He lights scented candles, their flames flicker alive,
Creating a haven of serenity where true love can thrive.

Glass of French champagne in hand, he kneels by her side,
Watching her soak in the bubbles of bath's tide,

Her smile reflects in the glass that he holds,
A moment eternal, more precious than gold,

Now the bedroom awaits, adorned just for her,
Scented rose petals scattered, their fragrance creating a stir,

Music plays softly, an ambience of romantic tune,
While shadows dance low in the glow of the room,

He pulls her to him, their hearts beating as one,
The night is just beginning, for the day is now done,

With whispers of burning passion, and promises deep,
They tumble together, a love theirs to keep,

The candles burn low, but their flame never wanes,
In a world of their own, they are freed from life's chains,

For tonight, they are bound by desire and fire,
Their two souls entwined, lifting ever higher.

Bikers

He rides the road astride his beloved thumping steed of steel,
For him the hands of time have slowed, the feeling of freedom so real,

Thoughts turning in his head, whilst his eyes ahead on the road, fixed in a stare,
He listens to the thunder of his motor as it removes all worry and care,

For him the destination is not the reason he rides on this road,
The bends and the valleys and hills and the feeling of awe as his ride has flowed,

He has no other reason to ride other than the love of his trusty iron steed,
The feeling of the open road and wind in his face blowing away life's pain and greed,

But the sad day will come when his journey must come to an end,
And loved ones and brothers will weep as from this life his soul will ascend,

Be certain though that waiting there for him on the other side,
Will be a brand-new, customised and uniquely personal ride.

A Lover's Verse

Why is it that when I am with the one that I love it is possible to talk the night away or share the sounds of silent conversation whilst wrapped in each other's arms, looking deeply into each other's heart and soul, with thoughts of her constantly roaming my mind even when I sleep,

Yet when she is not with me it is then that thoughts of her invade my mind and the feeling of being incomplete haunts me and leaves me longing for her touch,

Even when I sleep, she wanders through the halls and rooms of my mind as I float along behind her, watching her and following her trail of sweet perfume, wishing I could touch her, hold her, embrace her, and love her,

She has become a part of me, an extension of me and yet still separate of me.
Just as I cannot live without my heart...
I cannot live without my sweet love, any less.

SHADOWS WITHIN

The Loss

For so long you have been so far away from me,
Like a ship that is sailing away on the sea,

I watched with pain in my heart as you went out of view,
Those around expect me now to start my life anew,

But where do I start now, and how do I know,
What direction is it that I should now go,

You were my guide, my rudder, my sail,
Without you now by my side, I will surely fail,

They all advise, and tell me it will be alright,
But where do I head when all around me is night,

I wasn't expecting you to leave me alone,
And I really wish I could bring you home,

But you were taken from me, and I know not why,
Why God should take you, leaving me to cry,

It doesn't seem fair or right that he took you away,
Leaving me to mourn every night and every day,

How I long to be able to hold and see you again,
To be able to leave behind this tortured, gnawing pain.

The Man Within

Can I ask what you see when you look across at me,
A manager, a biker, an ex-cop, a poet, a friend or lover, or man of the sea,

Many hats I wear, yet none belong to the man so deep inside,
Away from view and deep in this body is where I hide,

Hidden away within my mind I try to find my life map,
But like the person hiding from himself, it won't just fall into your lap,

It is as elusive as a shadow in the dark that hides as if in night,
Always changing places, never in one place, yet it hides, in perfect sight,

If you try to get close, please don't think this is a game I play,
Should I suddenly put-up walls, or quickly lock myself away,

This tangled mess of confusion that lives inside my head,
Won't allow others close, and fears close contact with almost morbid dread,

So please do forgive me if sometimes my mind seems to wander,
It is merely my mind that locks itself away alone to quietly ponder.

For Kyle

I remember with such clarity the day you left,
Leaving my heart and soul, my whole life, bereft,

The call from the hospital, that beckoned me to your side,
Countless tears that ran down my cheeks that I could not hold or hide,

I sat their weeping, pleading for you not to go, helpless and lost,
I wanted you to stay so much, regardless of any cost,

I cried the whole time while I waited, begging that you'd stay,
But my pleas to God went unheard, and you were taken away,

Though only two short years you were in my life,
When you left it was akin to having my heart sliced to pieces with a knife,

Deep into my heart it pierced with abhorrent violence and great pain,
It cut a hole in my chest, that would never heal, and I was never to be the same,

However, as the years have passed, I have learned to go on,
But you are still in my heart, and though it's not the same, you will never be gone,

I'll never stop loving you son, none of us ever will,
Your mother and brothers, and those that knew you, we all love you still,

So please remember the love I feel for you and take care my heavenly son,
I still miss you son, and one day I when I see you again, to you I will run.

The Unexpected Meeting

You know that you love him, you know that you care,
He's the one that you married, your children you share,

You spent time together, precious moments of sheer joy,
He still makes you laugh, he still acts like a boy,

It's not that you hate him, or want him to leave,
The last thing you want is to hurt or deceive,

But his touch is now colder, he seems distant to you,
There are days when you feel inexplicably blue,

You go for a wander, now you're in a new setting,
You meet someone new, whose attention you're getting,

He came out of nowhere, like he came from above,
And landed there before you, with charm and poetic love,

It's not that he's handsome, rich or well-built,
He understands you, and like the flower, revitalises your wilt,

He listens to you, hears and hangs on to every word,
Whether it's spoken or not, somehow, he's heard,

With soft touch on your face, he disarms you in silence,
With his soft voice he ignites you, it just makes no sense,

He looks deeply in your eyes, and he gives a soft smile,
You gaze back and tremble, for it has been quite a while,

Since someone has touched, not just your heart but your soul,
And made you feel complete, not just a half, but a whole,

He knows he can have you, but he turns and walks on,
Leaving you standing and wanting, but now he is gone,

You think back on his words, his kiss oh so soft,
Who was he, you wonder, this man who appeared from aloft,

You go back to your home to another's touch icy cold,
You think of the stranger again, is how it will be until you get old.

The Memory

I hide an old box of memories under my bed,
Hidden away, but still close to my head,

Tucked away it lies there, hidden in full view,
Filled with memories of old, I may in time wish to review,

Memories of pain that I have deliberately locked away,
Visions in my head of times, that in the past should stay,

I fight the urge to free them, for some hold too much pain,
So, tucked away in their box, they must always remain,

But sometimes they escape, and why I cannot say,
All I know is that sometimes, they all come out to play,

Then one by one, in my mind they dance all around,
Screaming the most painful and depressing sound,

Causing my head to explode as my heart begins to sink,
As one huge regret deep hidden, comes out to make me think,

Of all the things I should have, or could have done,
However, the times when I chose wrongly, and then tried to run,

But memories though are faster than my legs will ever be,
For deep inside, one terrible memory still haunts me,

And whilst I have found peace with most memories in my life,

The pain of that one memory, still stabs my heart like a knife,

To ask forgiveness for this act in life, I can no longer do,
Till the day comes again, when I am reunited with you.

The Jerk

As a young lad, when first love strikes and you are still so young,
And the words you want to say, get stuck on your tongue,

When you adore her so much, but you don't know how to expres,
She flirts and through fear, you act like you could not care less,

When in reality, deep down inside you just want to take her to hold and to kiss,
But you are so awkward, and worried if you go to kiss her, you will miss,

What if you hold her and your member grows erect, and stands upright,
It has a mind of its own when you are young, and it would just not look right,
For her to see the lump in your trousers as they suddenly get tight,

What if she gets the wrong idea, that all I want is to get her in bed,
How do you tell her that she is beautiful, and you cannot get her out of your head,

Then you upset her one day, and away she does run,
Feeling stupid and confused, for what have you done,

All you want to say is sorry to her, but you really do not know,
How to tell her how you feel, and your love to her show.

A Father's Loss

An angel invited me today to go back in time and spend an hour with you again,
To feel your touch and hear your voice and try to rid myself of this gnawing pain,

How would I tell you how much you meant to me or how much I miss you so?
Knowing that I will never see you age, nor in size will you ever grow,

To leave you once more would certainly tear me apart,
And destroy even further, this tormented and broken heart,

So, this invitation given, though so enticing, I thank you, but I sadly decline,
For seeing you once more would merely start an all too familiar, salty flood of brine,

It would tear open the wounds that long ago I did try to seal,
Knowing full well that this was a wound, that time would never heal,

Slowly I head back to the path of my future that I am destined to tread,
My feet feel so heavy, my head pounding hard, and every footstep I dread,

For every step still rips me further from my memories of you,
And deep in my heart still burns a candle, for the son I still love and once knew.

The Truth

Like a hurricane you blew into my life, but I could not own you,
Yet you stayed for a while and created true magic in my life,
Happy times that I will never forget and will always cherish,
But then came the fateful day that you were called to move on,
You disappeared from my life and all I could do was watch as you left me behind,
I remember calling your name, but you could no longer hear me,
You had already turned your back on me and just like that you were gone,
Do you know how violently I cried, and how I blamed myself for your death,
Was it a cruel lesson that I had to learn or was it for another that you came and went,
All I know is that since you left my life has never been the same,
I struggle still whenever your memory crosses my mind again,
Times when you have lit a lamp in my mind and like a moth I focus on you again,
Memories of you sometimes screen in front of my eyes like a movie on a screen,
Bringing emotions to the fore that I thought I had long since buried and locked away,
But there is one thing that will never change, and this is still my resolve today,

I have never wished you did not come into my life, and would willingly do it all again,

For the love and beauty that you brought into my life far outweighs the pain of your leaving,

The love I feel for all my children is eternal and unconditional, unlike the pain I feel for your loss which will one day go away.

Leaking Love

Inside my heart there are containers full of love which I gladly share,

Which I freely give and share to those around me for whom I love and care,

But should they leave, and no longer can I share with those I love so dear,

Then these containers overflow and leaks my love from my eyes as a tear.

Questions

I have loved and lost love and felt the ragged, stabbing pain of loss,
My heart now beats much more slowly, with on a line it just won't cross,

Cracked and broken, patched and filled, there it remains walled up high,
I wonder, when did the stars refuse to flicker, or the sun stop rising in the sky,

When did the dark clouds roll over and the sky darken forever,
Was I wrong to love so deeply and without question, only to have it sever,

I am not bitter towards them, or remorseful, I am however pained though,
Merely wondering why it is that new love received, now can never grow,

I seem to go through the motions only now, not wishing to hurt anyone,
But my barriers do not wish to break, and I watch from window inside so glum,

Lost sometimes in a world so dark and bleak as I sit and ponder what I've done,

Till back I come once more to this world so full of beauty and pain,
To share the love, that I can still give, and share and care for others again.

The Final Ride

Alone he seemingly rides across the desert plains,
Heading to the light, as behind him the sun wanes,

He seemingly rides alone, you'll see no other,
Though he sees and rides with others that call him brother,

But you'll not see them, though they do not hide,
For they are with him always, riding by his side,

The dance with death he does with such grace,
As towards it he heads, though this is no race,

He rides on without stopping, he's not one to stay,
He'll ride till this journey will take him away,

Battle he must as he mines through his quarry,
If he has hurt you, then for this, I know he is sorry,

Please forgive this man, for he is plagued by a beast,
And he lost the last fight, when its strength increased.

The Fleeting Memory

That was goodbye my love and now you are gone,
My heart still aches, and I still cry even after so long,

I loved you then, I still love you now in every way,
I wish you every best, and if you think of me some day,

May you remember me as kind, and not with anger or hate,
One day our paths may cross, and we can wipe clean the slate,

We were not meant to be, and you have probably moved on,
Largely I have too, but I still think of you when I hear our song.

A Poem on True Beauty

What if beauty was scarred by one's own actions,
Unkind acts to others to your body brought reactions,

All the people we purposely harm and slay,
Currently they bear the price to pay,

We mock with our words those that we taunt,
To scar their body and in their mind we forever haunt,

But what if when we did such a thing,
To ourselves the scars and pain it would bring,

Our beauty would soon turn ugly and be lost,
For this would become our burden of cost,

To be judged as so ugly and for all to be seen,
As devoid of compassion with heart that is mean,

If only love could heal the scars of hate,
Would we all turn soon or would we wait,

Till so ugly we were, that all were repulsed,
And upon our site others gagged and convulsed,

Our putrefied ugly self so plain for all to see,
That we share not the love that is the only true key,

To obtain beauty within and beauty outside,
Or will our ugly self-remain because of our pride,

I for one will share my love and do my part,
To share the beauty, that I hold within my heart,

Not so that I could be handsome, or vain,
But hopefully to help others to ease their pain.

Cold Realisation

You took away my heart and left me but a shell,
I walked away so easily when, in reality, it was hell,

The pain I felt inside just tore me apart,
That day I walked away, and left you with my heart,

You told me that you loved me and told me that you cared,
We'd planned so many things that we could have shared,

But your eyes were glazed and cold that final day,
When you so easily just threw my love away,

You left me staring back in surprised disbelief,
For I would never would have thought of you as such a thief,

But you took my heart and just walked away,
Leaving me behind to face the cold light of a new day,

The scars are still there and the pain sometimes too,
Whenever I stop and still think lovingly of you,

I have built my walls high so that no one now gets in,
Try though they might I will never let them win,

My smile like a painted mask hides the feelings inside,
Whilst behind my dark, impenetrable walls I stay and hide,

But despite my feelings, I wish you no ill or pain in your life,
Though the pain in my heart still stabs at me like a knife,

Not hatred but love do I send and will continue to do so,
Till the day you release my heart and love lets me go.

The Mask

You wake each day as the sun begins to rise and you feel the pain,
For months every morning, it's always been the same,

You stumble and get ready, arming yourself to face the day,
You walk the street and people you greet with a simple g'day,

Your cheerful mask hides the pain that you've buried deep inside,
Like a treasure trove of forgotten feelings that over the years you still hide,

But lately something's changed, the mask is loose and falling away,
You try to hold it there in place, but it simply will not stay,

Your tears and pain are seen by more and more, each and every day,
And the feelings you have tried to keep hidden, keep bubbling away,

People reach out to help you, to lend you a sympathetic ear,
But your eyes are scarred from things you've seen, and all they see is fear,

You run towards the shadows to hide in the darkness once again,
The next day you wake once more and feel the same familiar pain,

But lately every day your mask falls further, and you simply can't go on,
For the light inside barely flickers now where once it brightly shone,

So, sleep my child your time has come, and I'll hold you close to me,
But this time when you wake in only light, and love and kind you will see.

The Beast Within

Here I am pushed down into this pit of hell once more,
But this time the beast now cowers and whimpers on the floor,

Gone are the days when I feared this ferocious beast,
Now I bite back, and when hungry enough on its flesh I will feast,

This Bear is a beast himself and know that whilst he's usually kind,
You poke him too much he will rip out your eyes and leave you blind,

Now he stands here seething with anger, rage cursing in his veins,
And thinks of ripping out their neck and watching as the blood drains,

His eyes now wide and glazed in what can only be a deathly stare,
Thinking of how he will pounce on them and lay them all bare,

Limbs torn away, eyes blinded, tongues ripped out, and hair torn off,
He'll tear you apart and you'll watch in a mirror whilst dying breath you cough,

Flayed of your skin and garrotted in part they will not die on first take,

They unleashed the beast and now must pay the price for their mistake,

Watch the demons around me run as I transfer my gaze unto them,
Be warned this is what happens when should you throw me down this pit again,
I will retaliate against you in calculated ways, so don't think me insane,

I'm used to the fall, I'm used to the thud, I'm used to the demons that come out,
They circle and growl and try to scare, but this bear will quickly smash their snout,

And when I am finished, I will walk away calmly and quietly into the new morn,
With you out of my life, cast away, while I walk slowly into a new life reborn.

The Returned Soldier

Together on bench across the park they look and stare,
One sees a sunny day and children laughing and playing without care,

The other sees only blackened fields with dead and dying everywhere,
One sees flowers and beauty, smiling faces with love to share,
The other sees the bodies of his brothers torn apart by shrapnel that flesh did tear,

One bathed in sunlight is the one they all see and have come to know,
The other is his shadow, he hides from the light and memories that it does throw,

Together they stand and both walk away together joined in their views,
One walks in light while the other hides in darkness, but both wear the same shoes.

Distant Shores

I stand on the shore and look longingly out to sea,
Sitting and wandering if you still remember me,

You've been gone so long, and times have changed much,
Yet I still remember your love and when I felt your sweet touch,

Your small hand engulfed in mine as we walked along the shore,
Running around and chasing you, and you always asking for more,

But that was a long time ago, and since then your ship suddenly sailed,
Though your memory is still so strong, and has never once paled,

Yet once more still I stand there, marching time in my mind,
And to the years that have passed I still find myself blind,

So, as I look out to sea, I ask myself why, and now where to and how?
For your new journey goes on, and I wonder where it sails now?

One day my ship may dock, and we find each other once more,
But till then your loss for me is still a pestilent pus-filled sore.

A Poem for Her

It's late, and I sit alone and think of her, and what she meant,
And realise that tomorrow never came for me to show the love I sent,

Letters we'd exchange along with calls and love so true,
But all that fell to pieces, and now my heart is blue,

It's been 7 months now dear, and still my heart is broken,
The things I gave to you, were far more than just a token,

My heart I gave so freely, for you to hold and keep,
But it all fell away the day I took that giant leap,

Great oceans crossed to see the one that I thought I adored so much,
Just to see your beauty true, and feel your gentle touch,

I let it go myself I suppose when I realised it would not work,
So why does the pain go on, and in my chest, still lay around and lurk,

I still look at you and the ring that I was going to give,
I wanted to marry you so that together we could eventually live,

I dreamed of a life together filled with love and laughter,
Where we could live happily in our special place ever after.

So now I face the world alone, and realize that tomorrow never came for us,
We both ran late and when we reached our stop, we totally missed the bus,

I've said goodbye to you, and still cried so many times,
I go through different scenarios still, and practise different lines,

It makes no difference though, and I know that love for us never came,
Tomorrow for me love will never come, for I feel I'm not the same,

I had a bucket of love in my chest, that once was overflowing,
But now it's beaten, cut and empty, and only rust and pain are growing.

The Game

Flying through life by the seat of my pants, I seem to give the impression that I know it all,
Skimming close to the ground, then soaring up on high, always with the chance of a crash or a fall,

Others stand and watch whilst looking on and gasping in awe, whilst some wish that they were me,
But I look at them and think, would they really, if inside of my mind they could see,

No instruction have I, nor any knowledge of how to fly, but I still always take the chance,
To make this life so much better, and hopefully the lives of others I can inspire or enhance,

But for me it is when the sun sets and night creeps in, that is when my nightmares begin,
In quiet of night, scenes in my mind are freed to play, whilst another within stares with devilish grin,

Where normally during the day I can keep him locked up, controlled and hidden away,
But it is in the night when I relax my mind, that this wicked part of me comes out to play,

With him he brings the memories of the past and taunts them against me one by one,
Reminding me of failures that I have had, and then blaming me for the death of my son,

But come the new morn, I shall rise yet again, and strap myself back into to my plane,
To fly joyfully again by the seat of my pants, knowing tonight he will come once again.

The Familiar Ride

Here we go again, that spiralling feel so familiar now to me,
But these days no one else can tell what I am going through you see,

The ride is never boring, and to those around me they cannot tell,
All the screaming in my head and the things these voices yell,

Tomorrow no doubt I will waken, and they will all be gone again,
But tonight, they have returned, and I listen to their pain,

One day they may defeat me, to end my tenure here,
For now though, I will just ignore them and enjoy a quiet beer.

Like Driftwood In The Ocean

I see you standing next to me and hear you talk,
Yet alone I stand for all intent, and on my own I will soon walk,

At night in bed, you lay so close, yet I am cold and feeling alone,
I know you love me, but it pains me to say that my love for you has flown,

In the day you bark your orders, and are always first to command,
Never offering once, or helping me, when I really needed a hand,

No harm I mean to you, and it's sad to say that my love for you has died,
Please forgive me, for there were many times when I really tried,

But your indifference to my needs, and your constant sniping,
Always on about the things that are not to your liking,

Have left me feeling cold, and I now feel very much alone,
Longing for the love withheld, that I so wanted shown,

Did you ever think of what I would want, or that I would maybe like,
Or will you always act so spoiled, and forever acting childlike,

For me it is now over, but please believe I am sorry to say,
Soon the time will come when you wake, to find I have gone away.

Angels on Earth

Here on Earth, there are two types of angels that walk freely around,
Treading softly to make sure not to arouse suspicion or make a sound,

Dark, and White angels, here on Earth, roam amongst us far and wide,
They both seek those forgotten, unloved and offer them a place to hide,

You yourself hide sometimes behind the mask of the dark ones, I know,
Inside of you I see the pain of your terrible secret, and I have watched it grow,

For like the mythical black rose, that lures with their smell so sweet,
You are trapping the unsuspecting for the Grim Reaper to meet,

Using your beauty to conceal all the thorns and barbs that you grow,
From those who are foolish enough, for your affection to know,

But I will always see you as you are in this life in which we both play,
No matter what costume you wear, or the character you portray on the day,

I do not fear you my beautiful friend, for I know all too well your game,
And I have long turned a deaf ear, when you have again called out my name.

Pushed Too Far

It seems that once again I face my enemies on every side,
Unlike the past when somewhere I would look to hide,

This time I will take some time to draw a plan and stand to fight,
To take them down by stealth and planning, combined with might,

Slaughtering them all, no mercy or leniency will I care to show,
Ensuring the speedy demise for any of my menacing foe,

They have all pushed me too far this time and I will win or die,
Never again will they threaten me, or into my life pry,

In mind and body I am ready, dressed and arming myself to kill,
They shall now be forced to swallow their own lesson's bitter pill,

Armed and ready for the fight, into battle I fiercely now do go,
And all that stand against me, or attack me, I will show,

That they must pay the price for causing my deep descent,
So on their deathbed, they may realize and sadly lament,

The time they pushed me that step too far, and I finally broke,
To the moment when they poked the beast inside, and it woke.

OTHER PLACES

Blowing Winds

Sails bellow out and carry me forward on winds of great change,
My direction has altered and new bearings I must now arrange,

The meagre offerings of the past are now just a memory of thought,
Of a life in the past where in a continuous monotonous loop I was caught,

So, if you are lost, then throw me your line, and I will gladly take you along,
Let me replace the moans of disappointment you hear with the sweetest song,

Cut your line at your will when you wish to be free, for our journeys must be our own,
Remember, plant your future well for time will come to reap the seeds you have sown,

My ship will take me onward, and toward to my final home at the end of this life,
There I will lay anchor, dock and offload and sever the cord as though with a knife,

Looking back across the seas I will reach and guide you through rough seas or calm,
To guide you to success, happiness, and safety, and before you, any danger disarms,

Till that day comes I give you my promise, that I will love you all, and help when you call,

Beside you, sometimes unseen, I will be the first to offer you a hand should you fall.

From Despair

Come taste the wine and fill your stomach to drown the questions in your mind he said,
Drink till all your worries and fears escape from within your poor tormented head,

You know deep down that it does not hold the answers to the questions you seek,
So, for now, it is easier to partake in strong drink, rather than to stand up and speak,

Your mind is filled with turmoil once more, but now joined by chorus of voices that scream,
Telling you to rebel against all those that stand against you and challenge your dream,

Your mind now swims in the wine that you have consumed, and inside you begin to cry,
Not for sadness or self-pity but for yet another dream that seems to have been sentenced to die,

You stand at its funeral, watching as it is lowered, and in morbid despair and you silently weep,
Another dream destroyed by the greed of others, merely so their power they could keep,

Slowly you turn and head to the place where solace you find, your only hope to move on,
But suddenly the silence is broken, and in blissful peace you find yourself as your mind does roam,
Surrounded by love, light and thoughts of peace, and loved ones that welcome you back home,

Awakened from the nightmare that has tormented you, you are safe and with friends once more,
Whilst there lying in state, still and cold, lies the shell of your old existence, lifeless on the floor,

Your time on that world has come to an end, and now your new journey is just beginning you see,
So much to learn, so much to see, yet already all your burdens are gone, you are now finally free.

The Cappuccino Sea

My life has been a journey, sailing on a cappuccino sea,
Master of my own ship, a ship crewed by only me,

Swirling froth lay before me with calmer waters deep below,
All adding flavor to my journey as onward I do go,

Good times I have are like the sugar, that adds a taste so sweet,
While the beating down of the sun above, shares its warming heat,

Along the way friends join me, like dolphins, birds, and whales,
All helping to guide and protect me, from windy squalls and gales,

I have travelled on this great ship since the day that I was born,
Starting this epic journey at the crack of an early dawn,

Yet one day I will finish it, and with it hopefully no regret,
When finally, the journey ends, sailing towards my own sunset,

But till that day arrives I will take pleasure and great glee,
To be so blessed to have been gifted, to sail on this...
Cappuccino Sea.

Together Again

*Today with an angel I did gently walk,
Slowly strolling along we quietly did talk,*

*About the past, the future, and the now,
Speaking of love, and hurt, and we discussed how,*

*When we were young how we would play,
But as we get older, we move slower today,*

*Her eyes still sparkled, and she smiled oh so bright,
And the flames of love still lit up her heart,*

*For to me she was just as beautiful in my eyes,
As on that fateful day we both said our goodbyes.*

Love Waiting

I watch you sleeping wrapped up in my arms,
Enamoured still by your beauty and loving charms,

An angel that was sent to Earth to play,
We fell in love at first sight, that's what they all say,

We've followed each other through thick and thin,
Sometimes we'd lose but most times we'd win,

We've picked each other up when one would fall,
We were there in a flash if ever one did call,

Now snuggled so sweetly as I lovingly embrace,
You sleep soundly in my arms as your dreams you chase,

I talk to you softly of the love that for you I still feel,
After all of these years, since first my heart you did steal,

For me you are still as beautiful as the day that we first met
And I pray that your love will continue for many years yet,

I love you so very much and need you by my side,
And every day the love I feel and shower you with I cannot hide,

So, sleep now and rest, and I will protect you my dear,
For you never need worry whilst in my arms I hold you near,

Tomorrow you'll wake and I know you still miss me every day,
And you'll wander why God had to take me away,

*But I am still by your side waiting and I wish you just knew,
One day you'll fall asleep eternal, and when you wake, I'll be waiting for you.*

Clinical Moment

He lies on the bed looking out at the light,
It swims all around him and bathes him so bright,

Figures of angels above him that flutter and fly,
He knows where he is, but realises for that he must die,

No memory has he from where he came,
And why in the light and not the flame?

The euphoria he feels brings peace and calm,
He feels only love and feels no malice or harm,

Across the light he sees those he knew waiting,
And hears the sweet voices of angels singing,

No weight he feels, nor a worried thought,
Merely the peace he has prayed for and sought,

He starts to walk towards his final destination,
But stops to listen to a shadowed figure's vocalisation,

No words he hears but sees visions of one,
A lad who still needs him, that lad is his son,

I cannot go he says, for my son still needs me,
Send me back and let me help him, is his only plea,

Suddenly back he is pulled with the force of a train,
Returned to his body so ill and wracked in pain,

*Now a whole new chapter in this story will start,
Awake is he not, yet from life he is still apart,*

*Laying in limbo not alive nor quite dead,
As a new journey plays out a new life in his head.*

The Reunion

She sits all alone quietly waiting for the one she loves to show,
Not knowing he's now walking towards her, for she does not yet know,

He greets her with a loving touch, softly brushing aside her hair,
She looks up to a loving glance, and it dispels all her despair,

A warm, inviting smile, a soft and loving touch to her face,
He lifts her up, and they begin to walk away from this place,

Towards the gate they stroll, by each other's side and hand in hand,
With a love that not many others will ever understand,

A love so deep, a love so true, it is indeed a rare find,
For in each other's lives their hearts and souls have become entwined,

She has missed him so much since she came here, and for him did wait,
For the man she so loved so much, outside this pearly gate,

Now back together again once more, they cross together into the light,
Where their love will now burn eternal and continue to shine bright.

Time To Say Goodbye

Sadness in your eyes tells the story that does unwind,
Of the pain and sorrow that I now leave behind,
Memories of the past flood in and fill my mind,

Battles rage on within me as I cry a silent tear,
While my heart hides in a newfound fear,
Tis the time that I must go and leave you all here,

For I have done my best and now can do no more,
Taught you all that I know, how to fully open life's door,
From knowledge I only learned when I fell to the floor,

During those times when I clawed my way back to stand,
When I could not rely on anyone's helping hand,
Times when I was drowning, yet still swam back to land,

These lessons I leave you, and hope that you learn,
That in life you can succeed, and then take your turn,
Not to crash or spin out or in fire to burn,

Now I look ahead to the one who comes calling,
Feeling myself lift, and yet feel myself falling,

I wonder what will happen to those I love and leave behind,
For I know how life can be so cruel and unkind,

I can only hope that they will embrace and take this chance,
To be greater than I was, and their lives to vividly enhance.

The Old Soldier

The old man stands alone in a foreign country on holiday and walks towards a memory of old,
He thinks of times and actions and his stories form a time that have never been told,

Alone he stands in fields of flowers and grass while his mind wanders back to an earlier day,
He watches the couples and families that fill the field with love and the children that laugh and play,

But his mind is far from this moment of bliss, and it travels through time to when he was still young,
Just 19 years old and fighting a war that took so many brave souls whose actions still go unsung,

He remembers the fear and noise surrounding him with the acrid smell of death hanging in the air,
Not a moment to think or rest, and always watching for movement with a thousand-yard stare,

Heavy is his heart as he thinks of mates gone missing and those he watched horrifically die,
Such a far contrast from this scene today filled with sunshine and beauty and a cloudless blue sky,

Pain and suffering for all involved as he thought of the many gone home still out of their mind,
He turns slowly and heads back to his family, but for a moment he sees those he leaves behind,

A tear runs from his eye as he watches in pain, his mind playing images of them as they fell,
His stories he still holds in his heart, and they shall always remain untold, for who can he tell?

Not you or I for we would know nothing of the feelings he felt, or the horrors he saw in his day,
So to all the brave souls who fought and have suffered I ask, please join me as I genuinely say,
Thank you for your service, may you find peace, and always find the strength to get through each day.

The Memory Train

The memory train pulled in today to the station within my mind,
Filled with thoughts and visions, there were some I wished were left behind,

Among the many memories I saw so many visions from my past,
Good times that seemed to go too fast and wished that they would last,

And times of pain, and suffering, and fears that chilled me to the bone,
Sitting side by side with happy memories as a child playing around my home,

So many carriages attached, stretched as far as I can see,
Filled with all the things that have come to define the person that has become me,

But then there appears one carriage that seems to glaringly stand out,
A carriage that holds just one passenger, and so I approached to see what he was about,

Slowly I walked toward him, my heart beating quickly as I got near,
A bead of sweat even falling from my forehead, as I felt a chill of fear,'

There I looked into this passenger's eyes and as he approached, I felt his cold breath,

Fittingly he came from the final carriage, for this passenger was Death,

He welcomed me aboard that train with him, and it slowly pulled away,
There I felt no pain or fear, just peace, as he spoke quietly to me, on this memory train, of the start of a brand-new day.

Midnight Caller

My friend the reaper came to my dreams again last night, and once more said hello,
He told me he was there for me, and then asked me if I was ready to go,

I asked him what the hurry was, and he told me that it was my time,
That soon we would be on our way, and for me the bells did chime,

Do not be scared, he said as we started off, and I walked closely by his side,
This journey for you is only a short one, though I guarantee you will enjoy the ride,

Then suddenly I was standing in lights so bright, in them I found myself fully bathed,
As the reaper turned and wandered off from me, and slowly turning, he waved,

Looking through the swaths of light, I saw, with such great beauty so as to behold,
Many familiar faces, there to lead me into this new world, where no one ever grows old,

But before I could step inside to join them, and in this newfound world to partake,
My ears and eyes were opened by the sound of my alarm, and I was shocked to wake,

Now sitting in my bed, visions of the peace I saw I still see, but tears now in my eyes,

For I still hear the sounds of friends and family gone, greeting me with their joyful cries.

The Cloaked Figure

Has anyone seen my compass I ask,
For I seem to have lost my way,

Where once I saw my future,
I now only survive from day to day,

A fog seems to have enclosed all around me,
And I am now completely unable to see,

Lost in this world I can no longer see,
Something is lost, someone has gone,

I cannot see my direction and feel totally lost,
Falling so fast, this feeling so wrong,

Clutching to grab onto anything I can possibly hold,
But I cannot grab what my eyes cannot see,

Spiralling down, unable to slow the fall I tearfully cry,
But I will overcome this fall and climb, or at least try,

Before this turmoil drives me totally insane,
For what other option is but to take hold and take a deep breath,
And learn how to deal with the figure that we call death,

For I will still try to win this gloomy fight,
To again watch the sunrise and defeat the dark night.

Answering the Call

*As we all go about our daily lives,
Like bees that buzz around their hives,*

*We dart to and fro, so focused on our goals,
While the toll of our chores burdens our souls,*

*But for the chosen the siren will sound the call,
Heard only by the chosen ones that will then fall,*

*Like a dream they will sleep and awake in the light,
To realise that Earth was where they lived in night,*

*All cares forgotten and now no pain do they feel,
In this new world that for now seems so very unreal,*

*They walk onwards to be greeted by others who left,
For a time of reunion to heal the feelings of bereft,*

*Now for them pain is over, and replaced with euphoric glee,
And for the first time their eyes are truly open to see.*

The Gatekeeper

Last night I walked again through the hallway full of doors,
Looking at those I had opened previously walking these floors,

They all hold memories, and all were unlocked and ajar,
For I had looked in, and returned from most of them so far,

But there at the end remains one dark door still closed off to me,
And while I know what lays behind it, I still sometimes long to see,

Last night in my dream I wandered up to this door painted a dark hue,
Only difference was that last night, I chose to open it and walk through,

In light surrounded I felt my weight fall away and all my pain leave,
But behind the door I heard the voices of so many that still grieve,

I wanted to walk out and leave to start the next journey ahead,
But the voices kept calling till they screamed in my head,

A cloaked figure walked over and embraced me with love and caring,
He listened to my tale intently and spoke softly to me, then thanked me for sharing,

Then he turned me around to the door, and sent me back through,

Explaining it was not yet time, and it was a time that he alone knew,

He would come for me and guide me himself to this world free of sin,

Where I could fly unencumbered and reunite with friends, loved ones and kin,

Now I stand here again in that hall, and look at other doors still to view,

Yet words still echo that I had been told, and when will be the time only he knew?

A Poem For My Passing

When I am laid to rest for others to say goodbye,
I hope that the friends in my life that I have made
Will want to come to see me that one last time,

And I trust that I will leave enough memories behind,
For stories of me that you all can share
And that you can all still talk of me with love,

Even though I have probably let you all down at times,
Before they carry my body away to be burnt,
Share the coffee and cakes and snacks that are provided,
For this is meant to comfort those who are there,

Feel free to shed a tear if you loved me,
If it is shed with love, and this is how I will take it,
But do not cry too long for this is not what I want,
For life still beckons you to live, to love and to share,

Hold me in your hearts during the party afterwards,
Celebrate my life in conversation with family and friends,
And fill your glasses and talk of me openly,
And dance and smile and do not be afraid to laugh,

At this strange party thrown for me when I am not there,
For in the future, I will ultimately be forgotten,
Yet despite all the tears, and despite any pain,
I want to thank you for allowing me to be your friend.

A Mother's Love

I watch you hang your head in sorrow and your heart is full of pain,
While your eyes, they leak the strength that you had hoped once to gain,

Your cheeks are hollow and sunken, and your face is gaunt and drawn in grief,
You call softly to her, but she is gone, and from the pain you get no relief,

Yet in the darkness from where you are I hear your cries, and come to help you heal,
And though I have gone and no longer see me, I know my presence you do feel,

When you look around the room, confused, you're sure that there is someone there,
Yet here behind you I stand supporting you my child, telling you I love you and care,

So let me heal your pains my child, and allow me to still protect and hold you near,
Allow me to soothe the pain that lives within your heart, and take away your fear,

A mother's love is never-ending, and she will always answer your call,
So I will mend the pain you feel with a gentle kiss, and help you back up from your fall.

The Message

Time stands still and light will fade,
Eyes will dim but they're not afraid,

Memories of those loved fill their mind,
The time is coming to leave them behind,

This journey is over, but others go on,
Though some may grieve now that they're gone,

For them this life will have no more meaning,
Unlike those left, now at the funeral convening,

Tears may flow, and pain may be felt,
But for them only peace is what will be dealt,

Can they comfort those left that they love?
When life is over, can they still see them from above?

Can they reach out, and gently cup their hearts,
With their love and care as their soul departs,

They still love you all and I will tell you this now,
It's just their way of saying sayonara or ciao,

So regardless of how your loved one may leave,
They've asked me to tell you please not to grieve,

Their love for you is eternal and will never die,
For love flies on through the heaven's endless sky,

And those that left leaving only a note,
Do not be pained for what they wrote,

Between this world and theirs there is no comparing,
But the love that you felt you'll always be sharing,

The time will come when again you will meet,
To hug each other with great love and happiness as you greet,

Till then continue to carry them in loving memory and in part,
In the warmth, caring and safety of your ever-loving heart.

The Return Visit

Last night you walked into my dreams and slowly walked around,
If I had not seen you, I would not have known for you did not make a sound,

You walked through, and opened the rooms of my memories turning on every light,
Softly moving to the next door when you finished, as you moved around last night,

I followed you to the darkest corner, the room at the back where I keep the most pain,
And I watched you walk in and shed a tear, and walk back out through that door again,

Then as you turned around you looked at me, and you gave me a gentle smile,
You walked over and hugged me, and then kissed me, holding me then for just a while,

We hugged me with such passion and love, and spoke to me, before you let me go,
And then I watched in tearful pain again, for reasons I cannot share and only I know,

As you turned and waved goodbye again, and you smiled and told me not to cry,
But that you would return again one day, and leading me, together away we'd both fly.

Glimpses

Did a fleeting glimpse of you I just see,
Running through the garden to hide behind the tree,

Was it you whose shadow I just saw,
Leaving silently through a hallway door,

I caught a glimpse of you I thought,
In the room where you were caught,

Playing with your stuffed toy dinosaur,
You just giggled and laughed and rolled on the floor,

I thought I heard you in my room last night,
Then caught a glimpse of you all dressed in white,

And last night I felt you and saw you at my bed,
I cried for a moment, since I know you are dead,

My beautiful son I miss you and love you so,
I call out and talk to you, and miss you dearly you know,

You left this world while you were still so young,
Complications brought about from heart and lung,

Everywhere I look I can see your face still,
For your death remains a bitter and painful pill,

Memories of your ready laugh, and your smiling eyes
But then standing at your coffin… to say my final goodbyes.

Quiet Thoughts

*A troubled heart and a mind so blue,
Sitting here looking out at the view,*

*One day I'll leave and empty my mind,
And leave behind a world so unkind,*

*But till that day comes I shall remain here,
And share only with those who hurt in fear.*

The Funeral

In the hush of twilight's breath,
Where life and shadows blend with the fading light,
We all stand at the edge of silence,
Embraced by the chill of night.

The echoes of laughter linger,
As ghosts of moments long since passed,
Memories whisper tales of the living,
And as these memories fade, the congregation holds on fast.

Beneath the ancient, watchful sky,
The ground, a cradle for the lost,
Where every grain of dirt represents a soul,
We all ponder the weight of death's cost.

With every heartbeat, a farewell,
The threads of life begin to fray,
In this tapestry of existence,
We weave with those we love, then drift away.

Yet in this solemn, sacred space,
Where sorrow meets the light of dawn,
We find strength in shared embrace,
And love will always endure, even though we are gone.

The Great Aussie Sick Day

I woke up this morning with a heck of a shock,
When I was rudely awakened by my alarm clock,

Get up it was saying, as it assaulted my ears,
Not good when your hung over from too many beers,

I should get up I thought to greet the new day,
But there in bed I continued to lay,

Five more minutes won't hurt, I thought to myself,
As I hit the snooze button on the clock on the shelf,

I won't go to sleep I thought, I'll just waken with ease,
To myself I did think, it was a thought that did please,

So there I lay in my blankets so warm,
With not a care in the world, I lay there in fine form,

But asleep I did fall, and when I awoke,
I looked at the clock, this was no joke,

I slept for two hours beyond what I should,
There was just one thing to do one thing that I could,

It involves some deceit it involves a good trick,
I would ring up my boss and say I was sick,

*Why waste such a sunny and beautiful day,
When I could just as easily claim for sick pay,*

*Enjoying the sun whilst wetting a line,
Catching fish for my dinner and enjoying a wine,*

*It's days like today when I love life so much,
Enjoying this sun and the warmth of its touch.*

Try Wearing His Clothes

He died today, he took his own life,
Leaving behind three children and a wife,

Word spreads and people start to say,
He looked fine when I saw him yesterday,

How could he do this they all ask in vain,
All he has done is transferred his pain,

Didn't he care, why didn't he think of us?
Why couldn't he just talk, and we could discuss?

It's so selfish of him just to leave us alone,
This is something we just cannot condone,

Was he sad, was he bitter, maybe he was blue?
If only he told someone who loved him and knew,

We could have talked, we would have helped him,
I'm angry he didn't come to us instead of committing this perceived sin!

All these things said, and questions asked, as they struggle for the answer,
For them it would have been far easier if he had died from a cancer,

But unless you have been there and felt his despair,
When you're so low and lost that nothing can make you care,

Whilst your life lies haemorrhaging all around,
And voices are nothing more than an indistinct sound,

No more can they see any future for them,
They are tired of fighting so please do not condemn,

Gone are they now and for them their journey is done,
You may not understand, but it happens to some,

So please hate them not, for their mind was lost,
And already they have already paid, such a terrible cost,

Life did test them, and on this occasion the bar was set too high,
So now they are among the heavens, somewhere they can fly.

The Tortured Soldier

In battle he stands but not for too long,
For he hears the tune of death's hallowed song,

Too long this war has raged on within,
Too long he's lived without giving in,

But now he looks to sky so bleak,
With withered soul for peace to seek,

Death's heavy stench of breath he inhales,
As onto the ship of death he sails,

First hurling pain, and then light so bright,
Death has now ended his mortal plight,

Now here he stands before a great gate,
But he cannot enter, for now he must wait,

Those who will judge him he'll come to meet,
Before he may enter, lost brothers to greet,

The ones he loved, the ones he lost,
But will this peace come at heavy cost,

Suddenly he feels a euphoric bliss,
Followed by the touch of a soft gentle kiss,

His heart becomes light, and he feels no pain,
Only love he feels now for the torment is slain,

He walks through gates and sees them all,
His heart overjoyed as he stands proud and tall,

He moves ahead but takes one last turn,
To look back on those mourning for he cannot return,

Though he knows that in time he will find himself here again,
To greet those whom he loved and now in Earth's covering blanket, are lain.

Blowing Winds

Sails bellow out and carry me forward on winds of great change,
My direction has altered and new bearings I must now arrange,

The meagre offerings of the past are now just a memory of thought,
Of a life in the past where in a continuous monotonous loop I was caught,

So, if you are lost, then throw me your line, and I will gladly take you along,
Let me replace the moans of disappointment you hear with the sweetest song,

Cut your line at your will when you wish to be free, for our journeys must be our own,
Remember, plant your future well for time will come to reap the seeds you have sown,

My ship will take me onward, and toward to my final home at the end of this life,
There I will lay anchor, dock and offload and sever the cord as though with a knife,

Looking back across the seas I will reach and guide you through rough seas or calm,
To guide you to success, happiness, and safety, and before you, any danger disarms,

Till that day comes I give you my promise, that I will love you all, and help when you call,

Beside you, sometimes unseen, I will be the first to offer you a hand should you fall.

From Despair

Come taste the wine and fill your stomach to drown the questions in your mind he said,
Drink till all your worries and fears escape from within your poor tormented head,

You know deep down that it does not hold the answers to the questions you seek,
So, for now, it is easier to partake in strong drink, rather than to stand up and speak,

Your mind is filled with turmoil once more, but now joined by chorus of voices that scream,
Telling you to rebel against all those that stand against you and challenge your dream,

Your mind now swims in the wine that you have consumed, and inside you begin to cry,
Not for sadness or self-pity but for yet another dream that seems to have been sentenced to die,

You stand at its funeral, watching as it is lowered, and in morbid despair and you silently weep,
Another dream destroyed by the greed of others, merely so their power they could keep,

Slowly you turn and head to the place where solace you find, your only hope to move on,
But suddenly the silence is broken, and in blissful peace you find yourself as your mind does roam,
Surrounded by love, light and thoughts of peace, and loved ones that welcome you back home,

*Awakened from the nightmare that has tormented you,
you are safe and with friends once more,*
*Whilst there lying in state, still and cold, lies the shell of your
old existence, lifeless on the floor,*

*Your time on that world has come to an end, and now your
new journey is just beginning you see,*
*So much to learn, so much to see, yet already all your
burdens are gone, you are now finally free.*

WORDS OF HOPE

The Unknowing Lighthouse

I watch you and my eyes see the struggles that you battle with, and with it the pain,
Your beaten stance reads of your troubles whilst your face shows the price of the strain,

My ears hear you speak of the despair, and your voice trembles as you tell me of your tale,
You think you are useless, a failure, but let me tell you, you are not useless, nor did you fail,

You were never alone in the storm, nor will it last forever, and soon the sun will shine again,
Calm will again arrive, and clear skies and sunshine will take the place of the clouds and rain,

May I take a small piece of your time to share some words that may sow in your mind a seed,
Of how these times are sent to teach us, and can then help so many others who may be in need,

Our paths in life are sometimes covered with obstacles that cause us to stumble and fall,
Your fall may even take you down into the darkest pit, where no one seems to hear your call,

Strength that lies within you will emerge, enabling you to stand once more, regardless of how sore,
It will give you the strength to enable you to then climb back out and find your footing once more,

And while you feel you were alone in battle, others have been watching you crawl out of that hole,

Giving them the strength and inspiration that they so sorely needed to help them reach their goal,

Do not think you have no purpose in this life or that you are nothing but a failure in everyone's sight,

For we all share times when we are the guiding light for others, and in doing so, help guide them through their darkest night.

My Thoughts

I have no more birthdays to celebrate I smiled,
For my time on this earth has come to a head,

From now on, please remember what I did with my gift of living,
My passion was for always helping, and to others always giving,

Cry not for my passing please, for all of us must leave this earth one day,
As for me I just tried to help others during my short stay,

But please just do with your life what you feel is best,
Be true to yourself and don't just follow the rest,

Make your life yours and give it cause and meaning to you,
While at it though, be the light for others and in their darkness shine through.

The Torment

I used to question constantly why they could not see,
The pain and suffering that they inflicted on me,

Times when I tried to talk, and they just shut me down,
Do they think they are GOD; do they think they wear the crown?

Why do they think that they hold this power over me, what is their goal?
But I have learned a lesson, something which freed my soul,

For I learnt to forgive in my heart, if not to their face,
And I let go of the hate, and discovered a far calmer place,

I do not tell you this not because it is easy my friend,
For the journey is hard, but the torment will end,

Only our own feeling can we truly console,
It is only ourselves, that we can we truly control,

Use the pain that they have inflicted on you,
To free others that come to seek, and for hope to renew,

For once you have won this difficult fight,
You will shine like a lighthouse attracting all with your light,

Peace will not be gained by revenge, nor fighting or war,
But learning to forgive deep down in your core,

Seek the peace in small steps, to suit only you,
And follow your lighthouse, till you have found true peace too.

A Caring Heart

Deeds and favours I give without cost,
Saving those that in themselves are lost,

No need to ask, no need to plea,
These are things I do you see,

No money expected, or favours I ask,
To help someone is a worthwhile task,

No reward is needed, nor praise to hear,
Tis reward enough to dry a stray tear,

To help you is but to help myself,
To share your load and share the wealth,

So, let me carry your burden and ease your pain,
For strangers or loved ones, I'll do the same,

Sometimes it costs nothing but to lend an ear,
To comfort with words and calm the fear,

Try to warm them when they are cold,
Or to assist them when they are frail and old,

Share a smile or make you laugh a bit,
To walk with you or maybe with you just sit,

I'll do what it takes to make you smile,
For you to forget your problems, if just for a while,

*Remember tomorrow the sun will rise again,
The night will pass, and the darkness will wane,*

*So, remember this even when I'm passed,
That pain is just temporary and does not last.*

My Offer of Healing

I watched you fall apart as you wandered through your life,
Watching in sadness as I see others take aim at you with their knife,

So many pieces I see fall about you, as you try once more to get up to walk,
Struggling with so much pain in your voice as I hear you struggle to talk,

Let me follow you a while and collect the pieces that you leave behind,
From those that have cut and slashed you, all whilst being so unkind,

Let me put you back together till again you are once more whole,
And heal the pain down deep within you, in your heart and in your soul,

Let me calm the waters in your mind that thrash, and bubble in turmoil,
From all the pain inflicted by others, that have made these waters boil,

Please allow me now to calm you, to heal you, and take away your pain,
The pain that eats away at your mind, that makes you feel you are going insane,

Do not hate those that misunderstand you, but leave them now to see,
For I will show you now just how beautiful life can truly be,

No payment will I take, no favour, nor request to perform a task,
For just to heal you and see you happy is all the payment that I ask.

My Life

Today I stood upon a mountain top and looked back across the view,
Places I had been, places I have travelled, and skies sometimes grey, but mostly blue,

I saw the rugged tracks and valleys with rivers long and winding, running through,
I remembered times I stumbled and needed help to stand, but all along I knew,

That this track was unique to me, and the pain that I felt I never tried to hide,
Memories I saw of those that stood by me, and those who today still are by my side,

I looked upon where I camped, amongst lush green forests where I didn't have a care,
To share with people that I loved, and we would share the laughter that filled the air,

I could still make out the sparkling pools of blue where we all would gather and drink,
The happy times together we were all still learning, it now seems it was over in a blink,

I could see the times of hardship, the tracks rugged and tough, ones that tested me so,
But looking back there wasn't one period along that track when I thought I would let go,

The journey that I took was different from the rest, and was unique alone to me,
To travel on my own path to experience and see the things that no one else could see,

Sure, they would see the sky, touch the earth, and feel the wind upon their face,
But just like a recipe, the ingredients we throw in give a different taste to every place,

I stand here now at mountain peak and see that it is down again from here,
Nothing bad in that though for this time it's on the other side and I'll travel with no fear,

The distance that I will travel is still unknown to me, but that's the way it's always been,
Don't ever fear the unknown, merely because it's something you have not yet seen,

And whilst my walking may be slower now with age, and it may take me a quite a while,
I will start my downward journey not with a frown or sigh, but with my greatest smile.

The Quiet Places

There are rooms inside my mind, hushed, hollow, and softly lit,

where no one knocks, no footsteps find, in the quiet pulse of where I sit.

Here, the world forgets to call, and time dissolves like mist at dawn.

The walls are high, the voices are small, the weight I carry is now gone.

In corners carved from childhood nights, they wait for me, my ghostly friends,

stitched from whispers, laced with light, with looks that know, with eyes that help me mend.

They do not ask, they do not leave, they do not flinch when my shadows rise.

They breathe the way that only silence breathes and meet me where the stillness lies.

And when I step back through the door, to where the sharp, the real, and the restless burn,

They do not beg, they do not mourn, but just nod and say, ..we'll wait loyally for your return.

Is It Fair to Dream You Into Being?

I build you in my quiet dark,

A sculptor, my mind shaping air,

Forming your voice, your steps, your silent heart,

But is all this just?, is it fair?

You do not choose the roles I write,

The walls I weave, the sky I bend.

You walk through doors of borrowed light,

A captive guest, a dreaming friend.

Do you feel the weight of what I make?

The echoes bending to my whim?

Or do you drift, untethered, unreal and fake,

A mystic shadow lost, a phantom dim?

What if when I awake, will you dissolve?

A mere spectre slipping from my mind?

Where in my head you appear and revolve,

Or were you real and I the wisp, of a fleeting dream you left behind?

My Life in Sail

The evening sea is calm and still, and the wind blows sweet and soft,
My ship her heading set for West as the sails in the light wind waft,

Behind me are the storms and hurricanes that once challenged me so,
But through them I bravely sailed, and forward and onward I go,

My crew they come and leave, and some withdraw when the seas got rough,
But this ship is mine and through stormy weather I'll sail, for I am tough,

My heading I know, but I will admit, my destination is a mystery to me still,
But on I sail with faith and strength, as I muster my strongest of will,

Whilst my ship provides me shelter and a means to take this tourney,
With the ocean supplying me the nourishment to survive this journey,

The day and night skies give their light and darkness to share with me,
Each one offering their own gifts and teaching to help me cross this sea,

The rain and the sun and clouds provide water and warmth and shade,
And all these things combined give me riches, greater than any man made,

This ship has brought me far on my travels and I know not when it will end,
But I do know that along this journey, I have met and made many a friend,

From casual to intense, from short to life-long, as well as those loving and true,
For all of whom are reading this, I have known them all, including you,

But there is one thing I can tell you true, that inside my chest I carry a part,
Of all my friends, my family and loved ones in a special place, locked in my heart,

So onward I sail into this glorious setting sun where water and sky both meet,
And one day when my journey is over, I'll be waiting there for you, with love to greet.

The Gift

Escape from your darkness and enter my light,
Leave behind in memories the terrible night,

Receive the warmth that heals your wounds,
Walk with purpose from the scattered ruins,

For far too long you were swathed all in black,
No love in your life, a heart scarred from savage attack,

But now with light and with warmth your body uncurls,
Like the sail of a ship that with warm breeze unfurls,

Or a flower that sprouts from the ground and bursts into bloom,
In all your glorious beauty and vision, you will stand soon,

Let me guide you and nurture you my beautiful soul,
Piece you back together and make you again whole,

Let my love for you surge through your veins and your heart,
Please allow me to guide and show you a brand-new start,

Then come with me and walk by my side and stay with me true,
And accept the love, wisdom, and peace that I offer to you.

Life's Wonderous Journey

Here in quiet solitude, deep within my mind's corridors and rooms, I travel quietly and ponder,
Of the many memories of my life, all still so vivid and strong, full of awe and wonder,

So much love I have felt for all those close to me, indeed, for each and every one of you,
Great pride and love I feel for my sons, my wife and my family, and the friends that I know and knew,

So many memories of both hard times and good, but all of them have taught me so very much,
I have learned to deal with pain and sorrow by moderating them with love's warm, healing touch,

Looking ahead, I know not what the future brings, but I will say with resolve and determination,
Come the time that this journey ends, I will leave with my heart full of love, pride, and divination,

I feel that we are here to gain knowledge and to teach, to impart the lessons we learn, and to guide,
Not just our children, but all those we walk with in life, and try to help all we can both far and wide,

So never feel that our lessons matter not to others, or let life's pain fill your heart with anger or hate,
For even though our journey is individual to us, from the lessons we share, someone may gain help from and relate.

A Poem for Lily

The child that was once, is now a woman facing the world,
And the lessons of adulthood, before her, are being unfurled,

New challenges she readily tries, and these she meets head-on,
Brave and strong now, she still retains warmth in her heart and soul,

Always trying to be the best in life is her vision and her constant goal,
She listens and comforts those around her who are feeling pain,

Tending their wounds and offering them the gift of hope once again,
She has heart filled with love that can be easily bruised and hurt,

Yet she has also learned to stand proud, and her authority to assert,
Lily I am proud of who you are becoming, and who I know you will be,

Though hard times will surely be sent your way in your life to come,
Remember that these are but lessons, and from them you must not run,

Take them on and learn them well, for all lessons will eventually pass,

And should you again be tested, I know you will be top of the class,

These words I write, I write for you dear Lily, and may they help you get by,
Sometimes in life we laugh and cheer, and other times we fold and cry,

Keep these words I offer you in your heart and use them as a guide,
For with love, and truth in your heart, you will have resilience on your side.

Thoughts of Hope

Here I sit surrounded by fog with many thoughts in my mind,
Wondering why sometimes why this life can be so unkind,

But make no mistakes, for I do not look back with fear,
And do not worry when down my cheek should roll a tear,

It's just a memory that's escaped from my mind that you see,
As I remember someone fondly that has long since left me,

But like a river that rolls on its predetermined meeting with the sea,
My one true love is still destined, waiting patiently somewhere for me.

The Healing

Let me hold you and wrap you up in my arms,
And against my body with all your charms,

Let me take away the memories and fears,
And let me dry your cheeks covered in tears,

Allow my hands to caress your body and remove all pain,
Then let me assure you that you really are quite sane,

Life has hit you hard and knocked you down,
Lately you have lost your smile and now wear a frown,

You have lost so much, and you feel it's unfair,
Is there anyone out there that can even care?

Let me extend my hand and my touch,
It costs so very little, yet is worth so much,

You are so valuable to many and so worthwhile,
And again, with help, you will learn to smile,

For the seed that I will plant deep within,
Will grow and make you strong once again,

A kiss to sooth and chase away the demons inside,
And a soft word to let you know you no longer need hide.

Prosperities Anchor

Why do we insist on tying our future to our past?
Is it not like sailing a ship with the anchor still at lay?

You prepare to set sail from the dock, and off you cast,
But in your head, skies seem always stormy and grey,

Then, despite favorable winds your ship still sails slow,
Dragging the anchor that in your mind you have cast,

Ahead the sun shines bright, but you will never move on,
Till you haul up that anchor, and finally let go of the past.

The Silent Conversation

I listened to someone's tears today,
And as they wept, I began to pray,

For their tears spoke of great hurt and pain,
Of people's spite that lashed out, time and again,

No words were uttered no sentence was spoken,
Only her occasional gulp for air when the tears were broken,

Her tears fell so freely and poured down like rain,
Is this what was her tormenters truly hoped to gain,

I went and sat with her, touched her eyes with mine, but never uttered a word,
But through the power of love, the thoughts in my heart were heard,

For she looked up at me and slowly there came a smile,
She received a feeling of hope she had not felt for a while,

With her eyes she said thank you and spoke volumes in kind,
And away she then walked with the new hope she did find,

In truth I wish her tormentors no ill will,
But pray one day, that love in their hearts will fill,

For love can heal without saying a word,
And love though silent can always be heard.

The Drums Within

When someone tugs on the strings of your heart,
And you hear the music, and the teardrops start,

It is just the memories of the beauty within,
That you recognise, and you set free again?

Too long it's been silent and longing to play,
Let it strum out its beat, and bring happiness I say,

Share it with all that have the ears to hear,
For this beautiful song is nothing to run from or fear,

Let the song in your heart, beat beautifully and soft,
And let all away all who hear it, be carried high up aloft,

For the heart plays always with such beautiful beat,
So let all hearts sound as one and let the tune sound sweet.

Ode To A Hero

A sailor of the world who's done our country proud,
Let's all give him a shout that lasts for long and loud,

A sailor of the seas who served proudly with our navy,
Sailing with many good men above the waves, whilst below dodging old Davey,

He willingly served in the Vietnam war, and proudly did his part,
A man who can stand proud and say, I served with all my heart,

When leaving there he did not rest or sleep,
But served our country once more, but this time law to keep,

A man of true integrity and chest that is full of heart,
In many people's lives he plays such a major part,

He still serves now but in a vastly different role,
Helping others with their lives, and lifting up their soul,

He helps those that are lost, with direction and understanding,
A man of true compassion and heart, and morally upstanding,

He gives so much but asks for nothing in return,
From this man there is so much we all can learn,

A diamond shining brightly to him my love I send,
And always will I be proud to call this man my friend.

The Hardest Journey

Have you ever seen the fog cover your path ahead,
When the mist that surrounds you also collects in your head,
You try to see where you are heading but to no avail,

Where you once drove down a mighty highway,
You can now barely make out a rugged trail,

Your head feels thick, your eyes mostly wet,
Stumbling you fall, your clothes wet and soaked in sweat,

Simple questions you cannot answer or respond,
And now you feel like you've landed in a pond,

It is deep and it is wide, and the fog is still thick,
Confusion in your head, the delirium making you feel sick,

Where is the shore now, where is the land?
Nothing can you now comprehend or understand,

You feel yourself sink and you think it is your time,
But when you hit the bottom, you find the fight to again start the climb,

Sometimes in life you won't find footing till you've reached the very bottom,
But upon reaching it, it becomes quite clear what has been the problem,

I will help you up, and be there for you with an outstretched hand,
But I cannot rebuild you, for this is your journey, please understand,

I will not leave you though, in fact I've been with you all the way,
And together we will travel till you again see the light of day.

A Poem of Hope

Do you ever get to a place where you just don't care,
When you tumble and fall into utter despair,
When the weight of this world crushes you down,
When you feel like you're alone in an ocean and about to drown,
You've fallen so far you can't see the sky,
For reasons you seek but, in the end, you just wonder why,
You've done so much good and put yourself last,
Yet still life hits you with an incredible blast,
Then I tell you the following because I have been there
So low that if I died at that point I just didn't care,
I learned to stand first, so I was not so low,
Then kept my head high to see where I wanted to go,
Take one step, and then stand there, and steady,
Make sure you were stable, so for the next step you'd be ready,
Take small steps at first, and steady each time,
For each step takes you higher as the path back you climb,
Look forward to a point, and aim to get there,
And when you do, the joy you feel you should certainly share,
Then set targets again, make them all small steps at first,
It's all-forward now for you've endured the worst,
Sometimes you might trip, other times you may fall,
But stand straight back up, and remember to stand tall,
It may take some time, and you may feel great pain,
But when the journey is finished, so much you will gain,
The journey is not easy as you make your way forward,

*But at the end of the journey lies a truly great reward
Never think of giving up, and definitely don't ever give in,
Keep following your path and celebrate each win,
And when you have made it, when your goal you do reach,
Help others who have fallen, so that they too can teach,
For if we all help each other, and let others know we care,
What a beautiful world it will be, when this love we freely share.*

The Secret of Life

Let me tell you a secret that sounds strange but it's true,
A great formidable secret that till now only a few knew,

Your life is mainly controlled by one person until you die!
This one person mainly controls it, you just comply!

They will take you here then they will take you there,
Without too much effort they will take you everywhere,

Who is this person I hear you ask, well take close heed,
It's the same very person that sits here, and this poem does read,

Yes, it is you who are the one who controls your life,
Not the police or the law, not even your husband or wife,

So do not complain when your life is not great,
Do something about it, for it's never too late,

Grab an idea or a dream and then follow it through,
And you will be amazed at just what you can do.

My Birthday Poem

Today I had the rich reward of reaching the age of 65,
An honour that does not come to all, and I am so glad to still be alive,

And as I travel back through my mind and revisit things that I have done,
I remember time of hardship and tears, and times of joy and so much fun,

For all that I have gone through in this journey, as I have travelled on my way,
Has helped me learn the lessons needed to get me through every day,

They are all locked away in memories now, that I can call upon when I need,
Like a book of life instructions, that I can always call upon and read,

And maybe even pass these lessons on to others who have not yet reached my stage,
To help them on their journey, so one day they too can share, regardless of their age,

Yes, for me reaching this age has given me gifts that hopefully I can share,
To impart on others that will listen, for my heart is filled with love and care.

Breathe

So, the ground around you has cracked and crumbled, and now away does fall,
You scream for help, but no one seems to hear, nor answer to your call,

Thrashing wildly, you instinctively run, but confusion rules your head,
All direction lost as fear takes hold, pouring over you with a familiar feeling of dread,

Breathe deeply and calm yourself, for it is never really not all that bad,
These are lessons sent to teach us, no reason to be scared, or sad,

Remember that while you breathe, you still have time to once more build again,
Breathe and fill your lungs with air to feed precious oxygen to your brain,

Shake off the stresses that leave you limp and concentrate to just breathe,
In time you will find that your troubles, will soon all begin to leave,

Tomorrow will come, and with it a new sunrise, a start to a brand-new day,
To rebuild again, and the offer of a chance to cast your worries away,

So, breathe my friend, and fill your lungs with clean and precious air,

It is the only thing that matters, and the only thing about which, you should really care.

My Life In A Book

I turned a page today in this beautiful book of life that I live in,
Stopping to look back on chapters long read, I can only sit and grin,

For times of pain and torment I can see only strength evolve,
Times of happiness and growth I see where my problems did dissolve,

Friendships with people, some still here, some have moved on,
Many of whom are still alive but some of whom are gone,

They all taught me lessons and some of them still do,
Some were fraught with lies, but most of them were true,

Love and romance I see scattered here and there,
As I remember feeling how love used to lift me through the air,

I loved all these women and in my heart some love goes on,
For each of us we exchanged our love until that love was gone,

Ghosts of some of those I have loved, haunt the pages as I read,
They come up now and again, and tears of sadness I will bleed,

My life has been chequered, with good and with bad,
With times of great happiness and sometimes the sad,

But no regrets do I have as I pick up my book and read again,
And I think to myself I don't know how my book will end, or where, or when,

But I am not scared, and I have no regrets, nor do I complain,
For it has made me who I am today, and, in my life, I have learnt I reign,

So, donning my glasses again so I can stay in focus I turn to the next page,
And it starts out that with me sitting, writing a poem on a computer of life's stage,

It begins; I turned a page today in this beautiful book of life that I live in,
Stopping to look back on chapters long read I can only but grin…

Angels

Angels walk amongst us, and lift us with a smile,
Stop and chat with you when you have been lonely for a while,

Help you when you have fallen, to get back to your feet,
They were that special friendly stranger, who helped you in the street,

That stopped to ask if you were lost, and could they help you along the way,
And made you feel so much better on that dark and gloomy day,

They helped you pick up your belongings when they all fell from your arms,
And the day you felt so ugly, they flattered you with their charms,

Yes, angels walk amongst us, and they are not that hard to pick,
For they are always helping the lonely, the forgotten, and the sick,

So, thank you to all you angels, for being the brave ones who dare,
To keep giving hope to so many, and to show that some of us still care.

SHORT STORIES

Undying Love

All around the lands were burning, scorched soil and bodies and blood littered the fields for as far as the eye could see.

Next to her lay the only man she had ever loved. His arms still outstretched trying to reach her, save her, protect her, hold her, but he never made it. Cruelly killed by a bullet just centimetres from where she was. On his way to protect her and shield her.

When did it get this bad, who started this war of death she thought?

She herself could not move as she too had been struck by the explosive fragments, and yet fate had bestowed it upon her the horrifying fate of having to watch the terrible outcome around her.

Beloved, man, woman and child shot down like wild animals and the earth scorched after them. She felt searing pain and with each passing breath knew that the end would not be far away as she struggled to breathe.

She looked around again everything was starting to take on a hazy appearance, she tried to focus as she lay there but everything was starting to get dim. Is this it she thought, is this my time, am I to finally be set free?

Her mind wandered to a time when she was happier. A time when her fiancée and her grand plans of marriage and starting their journey of happiness together.

She remembers the dress she picked out for the wedding and the songs that they picked out together to play at the wedding. She thought of the moment they met at the café when he accidently bumped her and spilled his coffee over her jacket and how apologetic he was. Even buying her a coffee and offering to pay for the dry cleaning. Her mind drifted again to the time they went to the park together for a picnic and how the ants got into all their food before they had a chance to even touch it. He was furious with the little creatures and all she could do was laugh. She remembers how he used to hold her and caress her head when she was stressed and how his hugs and kisses caused her to float to another world.

Never had she met someone so caring, so loving and so in tune with her thoughts. Able to take away her cares and worries with but a soft touch and a gentle smile. She remembers the first time hugged, and it felt as though electricity was going through her. It scared her at the time as she had never experienced anything like this before. He was always so gentle with her but still strong and masculine at the same time, she always felt safe with him.

Now here she was and her beloved lay lifeless in front of her, the pain was just too much to bear.

Her eyes grew dimmer and soon she lost consciousness as life began to slip from her.

Suddenly she awoke, and she was standing in a green field of long grass and flowers, their heavenly scent filling the air while birds flew happily through the air. The flowers and the long grass danced as the breeze gently blew. She felt no pain and had a feeling of euphoria. No cares, no worries, no schedules, or burdens of everyday life, it was magical.

There was a large bright white light before her and whilst it was very intense it was not painful to look through. She felt drawn to it and began to walk towards it.

Then in the light a shadow appeared and began to walk towards her, at first it was just a shadow blurred by the intensity of the light but as it came closer, she saw her beloved man coming towards her. She broke into a run, surely it was not him.

Closer she got and to her delight there he stood, whole and uninjured, smiling at her and setting her at ease once more.

They ran not each other's arms and hugged and kissed and just held each other tight. She felt safe again, safe in his arms and with him once more.

She sensed this time they would be together for an eternity, an eternity of bliss and love.

No words were spoken though they each knew what the other was thinking, and together they turned and walked towards the light, hand in hand... together forever.

The Veil of Night

The night was cold, and the dim glow of streetlights cast long shadows across the park. Emily walked slowly, her heels clicking on the pavement, her body heavy with the weight of the day.

The demands of others had drained her dry—endless emails, impatient clients, and a boss who seemed oblivious to her exhaustion. Now, as she made her way home to an empty house, the hollowness inside her felt unbearable.

At the edge of the park, she sank onto a worn bench, the metal cold against her hands.

She stared out at the moonlit grass, her thoughts spiralling. What's the point of it all? she wondered. She was always giving, always trying, but for what? To return to a home where no one waited for her?

Her sigh mingled with the stillness of the night. Then a voice behind her spoke.

"The night is like a silken veil that hides us from the next life."

The voice was deep, resonant, and startlingly close. Emily spun around, her breath catching. Behind her stood a tall figure, his silhouette framed by the faint light of the moon. His face was shadowed, but his presence was magnetic, commanding.

He continued, his tone calm yet profound. "However, there are times when your thoughts of darkness open a tear in the fabric of the veil, giving us glimpses of what could be… and what lies ahead."

Emily felt her pulse quicken. "Who… who are you?"

"A traveller," he said simply, stepping closer. "Like you, I wander beneath the veil, seeking answers."

Despite herself, she was drawn in. They began to talk, and what started as a cautious exchange grew into something deeper. His words were thoughtful, his insights cutting through the haze of her discontent like shards of light. For the first time in months—maybe years—she felt seen.

And then, suddenly, their conversation ceased, replaced by a silence thick with unspoken emotion. He reached for her, and she didn't resist. Their kiss was electric, a collision of longing and need.

They made their way back to her house, their passion igniting anew.

Over wine and quiet laughter, she felt alive in a way she hadn't for so long. Later, when they made love, it was tender yet intense, as though he were both grounding her and lifting her into the heavens.

Afterward, she fell into the deepest sleep she could remember, her body sated, her mind quiet.

But when she woke, he was gone.

The sheets were cool where he had lain, and not a single item in her home suggested he had ever been there. It was as though the night itself had conjured him from the ether and whisked him away with the dawn.

She dressed for work, her heart heavy, her mind whirling. Was it all a dream? It had felt so real, so vivid. Yet, as the day dragged on, the memory of his voice, his touch, stayed with her, refusing to fade.

That evening, Emily found herself drawn back to the park. She sat on the same bench, staring out at the darkness, her thoughts a storm of doubt and longing. She whispered into the still air, "Was it real?"

The night held its breath.

And then, from behind her, the voice returned, as deep and resonant as before.

"The veil has ripped once more, and again we find each other."

She turned, her heart leaping, and there he was, standing in the moonlight as if he had never left.

"Who are you?" she asked again, her voice trembling.

He smiled, a hint of mischief in his eyes. "Perhaps you already know. Or perhaps… you will find out when the veil tears again."

Conclusion

As we draw the final lines in this tapestry of verse, we reflect on the winding journey of life, with its peaks and valleys, its light and shadow. Through these poems, we've wandered through the landscapes of joy and sorrow, love and loss, hope and despair. Each page has been a mirror, reflecting the myriads of lessons that life whispers to us amidst its trials and tribulations.

In the times of trouble, we find our greatest strengths, and in the quiet moments between the storms, we find our greatest truths. The struggles shape us, the victories lift us, and the journey itself, with all its unpredictability, teaches us resilience, compassion, and the profound beauty of being human.

May these verses serve as a reminder that no matter how turbulent the path, there is always light to be found, lessons to be embraced, and strength within us to endure and to flourish. Life, in all its complexity, is our greatest teacher, and through its trials, we are continuously reborn.

With these final thoughts, we close this collection, but the journey, your journey, continues. Carry these lessons with you, and may they guide you as you navigate the ever-unfolding chapters of your own story.

Acknowledgements

To everyone who has walked beside me on this journey, your inspiration, belief, and unwavering support have been the foundation for this collection. Each of you has left an indelible mark on my heart, and this book is as much yours as it is mine.

To those whom I have written poems about and allowed me to use them in this book, a very special thank you, not only for allowing me to share your poem but for the inspiration you gave me to write it.

Also, a very big and special thank you to Emily Gowor and her incredible team for their dedication and hard work in bringing this book, and the one before it, to life. Your guidance, creativity, and commitment have turned my words into something tangible, something beautiful. I am deeply grateful for your belief in my vision and for making this dream a reality.

To my readers, thank you for allowing my words to find a place in your lives. Your support and connection to my poetry inspire me to continue sharing my journey. This collection is a testament to the power of shared experiences and the strength we find in each other.

With heartfelt gratitude, Ed Breedveld.

About The Author

Edward Breedveld is an insightful poet whose words resonate with depth and authenticity. His debut poetry collection garnered widespread acclaim for its heartfelt exploration of life's complexities and triumphs.

With his second edition, Edward delves even deeper into the journeys that have shaped him, offering readers a tapestry of life lessons imbued with compassion and wisdom.

A man of understanding and kindness, Edward has a unique ability to find the good in everyone, weaving this perspective into every verse he pens. His work inspires reflection, connection, and a renewed appreciation for the human spirit.